CHILDREN *of the* BIBLE

TWELVE STORIES

COMMENTARY
Stephanie Biggs-Scribner

MOTHER-DAUGHTER LETTERS
Stephanie Biggs-Scribner, Maggie Biggs-Scribner

CREATIVE INTERPRETATIONS
Linda H. Hollies

STUDY GUIDE
Minerva Carcaño

Dedications

My intention in this book is to emphasize the connection passed along from generation to generation. With that in mind, I dedicate my work to my daughter, Maggie, who represents the generations to follow me, and to my mother, Gainel, who represents the generation before me. I also want to express tremendous gratitude to my permanent partner in life (my spouse), Lee, who has suffered through both literal and metaphorical labor pangs with me.

Stephanie Biggs-Scribner

When I was seven, my grandmother, Eunice Wade, gave me my very first Bible story book. With it, she emphasized her belief in these stories as part of her faith, and by her life she had passed that faith connection to my mother and then on to me. I have fallen in love with the stories of our faith. My children, and now my grandchildren, have inherited these wonderful stories that teach, inspire, and leave us evidence that all of life is in the mighty and capable hands of the Ancient of Days. I dedicate my work to my daughter, Grian Eunyke; to her children, Giraurd, Gamel, and Symphony; to my son, Gregory Raymond; and to the memory of my youngest son, Grelon Renard, who is now a witness of our faith in eternity. May the voices of these children, who have spoken to me, now speak afresh to each of you.

Linda H. Hollies

Children of the Bible
Study Guide for Children of the Bible
Copyright © 2005 by the Women's Division. All rights reserved. No part of this publication may be reproduced in any form without written permission from the publisher. For permission to reproduce parts of this work, contact Copyright Manager, Room 350, General Board of Global Ministries, The United Methodist Church, 475 Riverside Drive, New York, NY 10115.

A publication of the Women's Division
General Board of Global Ministries
The United Methodist Church
475 Riverside Drive
New York, NY 10115

Scripture quotations (with the exception of a few rephrasings) are from the New Revised Standard Version of the Bible, copyright © 1989 by the Division of Christian Education of the National Council of the Churches of Christ in the USA. Used by permission. All rights reserved.

Book design by Hal Sadler.
Cover art and interior artwork by Melanie Reim.
Printed in the United States of America.

Please address critiques or comments to the Executive Secretary for Spiritual and Theological Development, General Board of Global Ministries, The United Methodist Church, 475 Riverside Drive, Room 1502, New York, NY 10115.

ISBN 1-890569-89-5

Library of Congress Control Number 2004116797

CONTENTS

INTRODUCTION

by J. Ann Craig

Welcome to the spiritual growth study on children of the Bible! Four special authors shared in creating this study. They invite us to explore a range of difficult, inspiring, curious, and even shocking stories about children in the Bible.

Stephanie Biggs-Scribner is a scholar of the Hebrew Bible (Old Testament) who provides background, context, and linguistic insights. We also invited Stephanie and her daughter, Maggie, to talk to each other about the stories in letters.

Maggie Biggs-Scribner was 10 years old when she was invited to share in this letter-writing venture with her mother. Her reactions give readers a child's-eye view of each Bible story.

The Reverend Dr. Linda H. Hollies is a noted author, teacher, and preacher who brings the stories to life with an interpretive voice. Her approach resonates with that of the Midrash, a collection of teachings by first-millennium A.D. Jewish interpreters who wrote elaborations on the Scriptures to glean more meaning from them.

Bishop Minerva Carcaño provides an insightful study guide to help readers deal with the fact that *Children of the Bible* is not exactly kids' stuff. We might wish our study to be a "warm and fuzzy" experience. We might want to learn how to read the Bible stories in this book to our children and grandchildren. These expectations may be fulfilled in certain ways, but in other ways this study may be as disturbing as it is comforting.

A special word of thanks goes to Susan Thomas for shaping this many faceted book through her editorial development of the text.

Children: Objects or Ethical Actors?

Children were often inserted into Bible stories as objects to make a point to adults. Even our favorite stories about children who became great leaders, such as Moses and Jesus, were written long after the fact to make a strong case for their leadership.

"But," we might ask, "what's wrong with that?" Nothing is wrong with using children as object lessons, but children are also interesting people and have their own perspective. Children's view of life is often overlooked because it is assumed that "they don't understand" or "they don't have enough experience." Yet engagement in a child's life can lead to an additional level of relationship with children—and with texts written about them.

Adults do need to assume certain ethical responsibilities to children, which include protecting them. Only adults can deal with the shocking realities of children without health care, children enslaved in prostitution or rug making, children who suffer obesity from a diet of French fries and soft drinks, children who are shot in schools. Adults owe a lot of oversight to children, but there is also a need for adults to relate to children as human beings. Because of the distance of time and culture, there are few models for such relationships in our Bible.

Moreover, while adults may be withholding certain information because children seem "too young" to deal with it, children are busy making ethical decisions in their own lives. Even in a "best-case scenario," adult efforts to protect children are often undermined by worldly influences on children from the media, peer pressure, and events such as war, unemployment, and homelessness.

Globally, AIDS has forced orphaned children to take care of other children. Slave labor, the sex trade, war, and poverty combine to steal all semblance of childhood from too many children. In African civil wars, child soldiers carry automatic weapons, and their survival depends on their willingness to kill other children as well as adults.

The most horrific experiences of children in our times may seem remote, but even children who do not appear to be troubled sometimes protect the adults in their lives because they think adults couldn't handle the truth. They are burdened with assaults, peer pressures, family secrets, or health issues that would challenge any adult. We might hear these stories in snippets, but we must guess at the details. Likewise in the Bible, the stories of children are often sketchy.

Linda H. Hollies provides a model for reading between the lines—both of Scripture and of children's lives—so that we can imagine the voices of the young people. The children in the Bible had a context of their own, but we hear their stories through the voices of adults. No wonder there is a multitude of missing details. Are we hearing the voices of the children of our own day?

Listening to One Child: Maggie at 10

In our study book, we hear the voice of the young Maggie Biggs-Scribner, who responds in her own words to the range of inspiring, strange, and troubling stories in this book. Her contributions raised some interesting issues.

Every year, manuscripts of our spiritual growth study are reviewed before publication by directors and staff of the Women's Division. Some reviewers thought that Maggie sounded much younger than 10. Others thought that someone older had written her letters for her. Maggie will tell you that she wrote them herself.

We have to realize that we rarely read the published words of children or young people of our own day. This is an unusual opportunity. Observe your own reactions to Maggie's letters. We, too, are not used to treating children as full people.

In the first full edit of the manuscript, which included Maggie's letters, Maggie's name was left off the title page. It's easy for us to let children and young people disappear— even as we try to advocate for them.

Ways to Read This Book

Finally, reading this book will be an adventure with optional approaches. Each story about children is told three different ways. When an important story is communicated in the Bible, it is often told more than once and in more than one way. The best example is the four Gospels, but this strategy is found throughout the Scriptures.

Stephanie Biggs-Scribner gives us each story with historical and linguistic insights. Then Stephanie and Maggie discuss the story in a mother-daughter dialogue. Finally, Linda H. Hollies presents one way of fleshing out the story from the skeleton of information we have.

You may enjoy reading the book straight through, or you could read all the letters first, or you might prefer to focus on the Midrash stories by Linda. You could start with the background information in the Prologue and Epilogue, or you could plunge right into a story that interests you. You are invited to be your own "tour guide." If you plan to use this book at a three-day event, it can be conveniently divided into three units by studying the Prologue with the four stories of Part I, the five stories of Part II as a unit, and the three stories of Part III with the Epilogue.

Whatever approach you take to the text, keep in mind that you were once a child. Remember your own childhood through the stories.

Remember the adults who made a difference for better or for worse. In the Bible there are both joyous and painful stories, just as in our own lives. When you cheer or weep for children in the Bible, remember that Christ would have each of us become like a child. He called us to be born again—to become newborns. It makes sense to understand *Children of the Bible* and the children in our lives as keys to a new dimension of faith.

PROLOGUE

LIFE SIGNS OF A PEOPLE

by Stephanie Biggs-Scribner

In an age when parenting has become a best-selling topic, why do we not see the shelves of bookstores lined with books about children in the Bible? There are many such stories. People raised in church-school classes can usually list a number of them, such as the stories of the baby Moses, David and Goliath, and the healing of Jairus's daughter, to name a few. Considering the familiarity of such stories, it is surprising that the opportunity for adults to study them rarely comes along.

Perhaps opportunities to study Bible stories about children are rare because of an assumption by adults that they already know all there is to know about children in the Bible. Or perhaps it is because adults think the topic is "childish." However, it is more likely that opportunities to study children in the Bible are rare because of the numerous problems involved. These include:

- A lack of details in many of the stories.
- The presence of disturbing details in other stories.
- The difficulty of coming up with a basic definition of what or who is a child in the Bible.
- The difficulty of selecting the texts one intends to use.

Studying children's roles in the Bible can be a profound experience for readers. In fact, children in the Bible stories often serve as "life signs" through which the quality or status of the life of a community is revealed. Reading the stories of children in the Bible through the lens of life signs could heighten our awareness of the impact of children; but because of the difficulties encountered when reading children's stories, a strategy for reading them is necessary. We begin by elaborating on these difficulties and explaining how we will approach them.

A Lack of Details

One difficulty in studying children in the Bible is that many of the stories leave important questions unanswered. For instance, what was Ishmael doing when Sarah became angry and sent him away (Genesis 21:9-14)? What was the childhood of Moses like (Exodus 2)? What kind of childhood did Jesus have (Luke 2)? Frustratingly, answers to such questions will probably never be known. Yet studying these texts allows us to learn much about children in the Bible and encourages us to imagine possible answers to the questions we ask.

In order to arrive at the fullest possible understanding of what the Scriptures said, ancient Jewish rabbis elaborated upon what they found in the Torah by applying it to hypothetical cases from daily life. A compilation of their teachings from 400 B.C. throughout and beyond the first millennium is referred to as the Midrash. In the series of "Different Views" found in this book, the Reverend Dr. Linda H. Hollies elaborates, in the style of a modern Midrash, on the Bible stories we have chosen to study. Missing information, such as what motivates the characters and how they are feeling, is supplied from the viewpoint of a child who is a character in the story. The creative interpretations written by Dr. Hollies reveal one writer's struggle to arrive at a personal application of the text. This type of participation in the biblical tradition helps to keep the tradition alive and brings it to life within us.

The Presence of Disturbing Details

An example of a story with disturbing details is the passage about Jephthah's sacrifice in Judges 11. To repay God for giving him a victory, Jephthah vowed to make a burnt offering of the first thing that came out of his house when he returned home. The first "thing" to come out of his house happened to be his daughter. Among questions this story might stir are:

- Why did Jephthah make such a rash vow?
- Did he think he was sacrificing his daughter's body as an offering to God?
- Was God pleased with Jephthah for keeping his vow?
- Why does the story fail to name the daughter, even though her sacrifice was commemorated with a yearly celebration?

Although answers to such questions about Jephthah's daughter will not be found in this book, the story will be discussed at length.

Defining the Term "Child"

In the times described in the Bible, who or what was a child? When did adulthood begin? Childhood probably ended earlier in the cultures that developed the Bible stories than in modern First World societies. Even as recently as the eighteenth century, children were considered "small adults."[1] Families often depended upon all members of the household—children included—to support and sustain the family unit.

The Bible contains texts that were generated by different peoples in a number of different times and situations. No doubt, the understanding of what childhood was fluctuated during the span of time when the texts were generated. Moreover, the Bible never offers a straightforward definition of the term "child" for any community in any time frame. Perhaps the terms for "baby," "child," and

so forth were so well understood by the authors and original hearing communities that explanations were considered unnecessary. Therefore, determining who is and who is not a child in a Bible story is not an objective task. Birth certificates and other such documents that could determine who and what a child was in Bible times do not exist. Ages are not announced. Determining who is a child must be done by context and is a subjective matter.

For example, how old were Cain and Abel? The context tells us they were old enough to be doing adult tasks such as farming and herding. They were also old enough to do abstract theological thinking about sacrifices acceptable to God. Yet in the story they exemplify the vying for approval typical of children. Since they exhibit both adult and childish behaviors, we might deduce that they are adolescents. In the story of Jephthah's daughter (Judges 11), we must deduce her age from her degree of spontaneity and the fact that she and her friends are allowed to go into the mountains alone.

Selecting Texts

A major challenge to studying children of the Bible is deciding which stories and which sources to use as we explore the subject. In the case of this book, the Hebrew Bible and the Greek New Testament are the starting places for study. Some references to the *Koran* and to other ancient Jewish and Christian sources will be made when they are applicable to the stories chosen for this study.

Even though we narrow our selection of stories to the Protestant Bible, we are left with the difficulty of addressing a substantial amount of material. There are so many stories of children that discussing all of them would fill a far larger book than the one at hand. In this book, the strategy will be to choose 12 stories about children and to analyze them in detail, one at a time.

A letter from me to my 10-year-old daughter, Maggie, about each story and her response to me will follow the opening analysis. Maggie and I have decided to share in this way so that others may benefit from our communications. After the letters will come "A Different View" of each story, a creative interpretation provided by Dr. Hollies. The 12 stories will be grouped into three Parts:

Part 1: Children in Troubled Families
Part 2: Children under Threat
Part 3: Children Who Show Enterprise

Not all of the stories we present may deal with the particularities of childhood or the questions about child raising that twenty-first-century readers would like to have addressed. Often, Bible stories about children do not tell us much about their young lives. Instead, they seem to replace our common image of "childishness" with adult concerns. It is as if the biblical text does not let children remain children for long. Also, the prevalence of violence in the stories about children in the Bible may disturb rather than inspire readers. Sometimes this means that stories send us jolts of shock and wake us up. Perhaps jolts such as this are meant to make us "hear" the stories with more attentive ears or to encourage us to think about them long and hard.

A stratagem for dealing with these problems is to bear in mind that the stories were not written during our time or within our culture. This means that these stories will not always be stories we would like to share with young children. As a matter of fact, thinking of the Bible as having been written *primarily* for adults, and secondarily for adults to share with children as they grow up, will prevent unrealistic expectations.

Although our study of children in the Bible is complex, a keen reading of the stories is not impossible and has profound payoffs. The continued life of our species requires the procreation and careful raising-up of children. The lives of parents, grandparents, and teachers of children revolve around children on a daily basis. For generations this has been the case. Getting to know more closely the stories of children in the Bible offers an opportunity to consider how well we may have cared for our "life signs" of hope—our children.

INTRODUCTORY LETTERS

by Stephanie and Maggie Biggs-Scribner

Dear Maggie,

I know we don't write letters to each other very often, so it might seem weird to get a letter from me now. But I have something I hope we can do with this letter, if you are willing. It won't be easy, so I want to explain it to you. I would like to write you letters about some of the stories about children in the Bible. And I would like for you to write me back and tell me what you think about them. Let me explain to you that there are two reasons why it might not be easy for us to share in this way. One reason is that the stories aren't always nice. Kids are in the stories and they are in the Bible, but that doesn't mean they are always happy. Sometimes the stories are sad or even scary. We can't prove they really happened just the way we tell them, but they are in the Bible for a reason. You see, sometimes a story can be "true" because it teaches us something worth thinking about, such as how not to treat each other. Does that make sense?

The second reason that it might not be easy for us to write each other about these stories is that, when we are done, I would like for us to share our letters with other people by putting them in a book. It may be exciting to think about putting our letters together into a book to publish them, but I want you to think about it carefully. Imagine . . . if we put our letters into a published book, it will be around for a long time. You will grow up and become an adult. You will change a lot as you grow, but this book containing what you thought about some Bible stories when you were a kid will not have changed. It's good for you to change your mind about things, as you probably will about these stories, but the book won't change once it is printed. It won't show how you have grown. And when people read it, they will be people that you and I don't even know! It is a big decision to do this.

Maggie, if you think this is too weird to do and you don't want to write about these stories, I will understand. I love you no matter what you decide. As I said before, some of the stories are not stories that we may like. In fact, I would not be willing to share some of them with you if you were a few years younger—not all of them are meant for younger kids. But all of them are supposed to make us think. If you do not want us to share our thoughts with each other this way, it will be okay. Just let me know if you want to try this or not.

Love always,
Mom

Dear Mom,

Yes, I would love to write letters to you. For more than one reason, I wish to know more about the Bible, or understand it more. Like David and Goliath—yeah I get the concept, boy kills giant with slingshot, but I don't get the meaning of the story. I think if I do this, I will understand it in a way I don't right now!

Love,
Maggie

Part 1

CHILDREN IN TROUBLED FAMILIES

CAIN & ABEL

(GENESIS 4:1-16)

Troubled family relations figure in numerous stories of children in the Bible. In Genesis alone we find the stories of Cain and Abel, Ishmael and Isaac, Esau and Jacob, Rachel and Leah, and Joseph and his brothers. These stories share similar characteristics, such as the issue of sibling rivalry, that provide "continuity across the whole of Genesis." [2]

The story of Cain and Abel tells of a terrible event that is responded to not by the parents of the siblings but only by God. We don't know the ages of Cain and Abel when the murder of Abel takes place, but we do know that the brothers function as children to Adam and Eve and that the tragic outcome of the competition between them is an example of what can happen when sibling rivalry is allowed to go unchecked by parents. Since the story seems to tell of the first sacrifice of the products of their labor—a sacrifice that the boys are making on their own—it is plausible that they are young teenagers with the bodies of strong adolescents and the minds of children. Today we might call Cain a troubled youth.

In this story, there are numerous ironies. The ironies to be discussed here involve the names of the sons, the parents' roles, and God's role. Eve gives birth to two sons: first Cain and then Abel. Cain's name is a wordplay for having been "acquired" from God (Gen. 4:1). Though the text does not attribute any meaning to Abel's name, it may also be a wordplay. His name is the same as a word used over and over in Ecclesiastes, which is translated in the New Revised Standard Version as "vanity." It could also be translated as "ephemerality." In other words, his name does not express the same gratitude to God that his brother's name expresses. Rather, his name foreshadows his fleeting, ephemeral existence.

Naming children is typically the job of the parents. In this story, Eve is the one who names Cain, but Abel's name is not attributed to either parent. If Abel's name does indeed foreshadow his early death, then the role of parents in carefully selecting names for their children has profound consequences. For lack of being carefully named, Abel suffers the fate of having no future. Viewed from the perspective of name giving, the neglect of the parents in this story is fatal. It must be said in their defense, however, that Adam and Eve were the Bible's first parents. They did not have the benefit of experienced relatives or books by child-rearing experts to help them deal with a phenomenon that had not even been named yet—sibling rivalry.

Commentary
by Stephanie Biggs-Scribner

Now Abel was a keeper of sheep, and Cain a tiller of the ground. In the course of time, Cain brought to the LORD an offering of the fruit of the ground, and Abel for his part brought of the firstlings of his flock, their fat portions. And the LORD had regard for Abel and his offering, but for Cain and his offering he had no regard. So Cain was very angry, and his countenance fell. The LORD said to Cain, "Why are you angry, and why has your countenance fallen? If you do well, will you not be accepted? And if you do not do well, sin is lurking at the door; its desire is for you, but you must master it.

Cain said to his brother Abel, "Let us go out to the field." And when they were in the field, Cain rose up against his brother Abel, and killed him. Then the LORD said to Cain, "Where is your brother Abel?" He said, "I do not know; am I my

brother's keeper?" And the LORD said, "What have you done? Listen; your brother's blood is crying out to me from the ground! And now you are cursed from the ground, which has opened its mouth to receive your brother's blood from your hand. When you till the ground, it will no longer yield to you its strength; you will be a fugitive and a wanderer on the earth."
(Gen. 4:2b-12)

What of God's role in this story? Why does the story portray God as preferring Abel's offering to Cain's? It is hard to imagine God as playing favorites. Moreover, considering the fact that Genesis has mentioned only food from trees (Gen. 2:16) and does not mention food from animal sources until the time of Noah (Gen. 9:3), it is difficult to make sense of why God's favorite—if God had to choose favorites—would be Abel, the shepherd who offers an animal!

This text does not suggest easy answers to such difficulties as the importance of names, the role of parents, and God's role. Rather, readers must struggle with topics like these. Certainly the story does lay the groundwork for the later sibling rivalries that readers of the Hebrew Bible are likely to encounter. And the story gives the first indication of the importance God assigns to blood sacrifice, a theme that recurs all the way through the Bible up to the shedding of Christ's blood to take away the sins of the world.

LETTERS ON THE STORY OF CAIN AND ABEL

by Stephanie and Maggie Biggs-Scribner

Dear Maggie,

Our first story is sad, because it is about two brothers who don't do things the same way. One brother, Abel, is a shepherd, and the other brother, Cain, is a gardener. When the two of them give offerings to God, Cain gives some of the fruit and vegetables he has grown, and Abel gives some of his best sheep. The story says that God pays attention to Abel, but not to Cain. Cain is mad about that. God says to Cain that he would win approval if he did good things. But, instead of trading some of his vegetables for a lamb to sacrifice, Cain gets Abel to go out into a field with him, and he kills Abel!

Since you don't have any brothers or sisters, this story must be hard to imagine. But you do have lots of friends with brothers and sisters, and you know how mad they can get at them! Plus, you know how annoyed you can get at people after spending lots of time around them. Think about the last time you were mad at somebody—anybody. We all get mad. I think the Cain and Abel story is supposed to make us consider what we do when we get mad. I hope you never get so mad that you want to hurt somebody. In fact, one of the tenets of the Tae Kwon Do we are learning is self-control. That's very important. Master Keith sometimes asks what is hardest for each of us. I think Cain's biggest challenge is controlling his temper. Tae Kwon Do helps me feel more self-confident, and when I am confident, I can control my feelings and my actions better.

I have to admit, though, I do need to work on controlling my tongue. Too often when my feelings are hurt, I say things I regret later. That will be something I will work harder on. What about you? What do you feel like you need to work on?

Love,
Mom

11

Dear Mom,

I think Cain will soon regret what he did! After all it was his brother he killed. I can't imagine hating someone so much that I'd kill them.

My tongue does get out of control sometimes and I say things to people just because they get on my nerves. You know how at school there is always someone you don't like? Well, most of the time I'm able to ignore them, but sometimes I blurt something out I probably shouldn't.

Love,
Maggie

A DIFFERENT VIEW: CAIN AND ABEL *By Linda H. Hollies*

My blood runs along the earth. My blood stains the hands of my own brother. My blood continues to speak from the very dirt that the first parents were made of "in the beginning"! My blood begs to be heard. My blood has a message for the world. My blood will one day be avenged, for life is in the blood.

I know that my brother did not intend to kill me, for that would not have changed God's mind about the power of blood as a sacrifice. My brother, Cain, was filled with rage, but it was rage at God! I was only his innocent victim. The vio-lence Cain began continues to this day. Seldom is there a good reason for killing another human being. We are a family, created of one blood, from one set of parents. It's rage that makes us insane. It's rage that drives us to take matters into our own hands. Cain did not have control over his hateful emotions. He was in a state of rage when he killed me.

Cain was the oldest son of our parents, Adam and Eve. Our mother was so very proud of her first baby that she exclaimed, "I have gotten a man from God!" You have to remember that my parents were made, created, and formed from the dust of the earth! It was only after the Creator breathed into their nostrils that they began to experience the blood running warm in their veins!

When my parents had rebelled against God in the Garden of Eden, they tried to make some clothes out of fig leaves to cover their nakedness. God came in the cool of the evening and said to Adam and Eve, "Where are you?" The question did not mean that God could not find them but that their relationship with their Creator had been ruptured! Because of this, innocent animals had to be sacrificed throughout the ages to make up for my parents' sin. And God took the skin from the first animal sacrificed and made my parents coats to protect them from cold outside the Garden.

With this act of loving mercy, God instituted the law that "without the shedding of blood there is no forgiveness of sins." (Hebrews 9:22b) It was not my fault Cain was kept closer to home by our mother. He was her firstborn, her favorite. He worked with her to learn to till the soil and grow abundant crops. He was an excellent farmer.

I was the baby of us two. Dad was determined that one of us would keep him company and learn how to do the hunting and the herding, so I became the one. I was skilled with the flocks. Each of us boys had a specialty. And each of us had been taught to offer a sacrifice unto God.

Cain and I didn't have too many arguments in our earlier days. I never sensed rage in my brother then. Our family worked as a unit. We worked hard, and the hours were long. When Cain and I finished our work, we were tired. We ate dinner as a family. We prayed together. Soon we were all asleep, awaiting the sunlight.

One day we both stopped at the family altar about the same time. You should have seen the huge basket of fresh-grown fruits and vegetables Cain laid upon the altar. The fruits looked luscious, and the vegetables had a lingering odor of the good earth clinging to them. Cain really knew how to work the land.

I waited until he had made his sacrifice, and then I presented the firstborn animals from my flocks. Of course, they had to be killed. Their blood ran all over the altar, and the smell of it was very strong. God was pleased with my offering. Cain's feelings got hurt. I didn't say a word. I was not asking God to make me a favorite! I was just offering my thanksgiving sacrifice as I'd been taught.

Cain and God had a long conversation. Don't ask me to give you details. I just know that Cain never came in for dinner that night. There was a lot of tension around the pots over the fire. It was the very first time that we had not eaten together as a family. I tried to wait up for Cain, but finally I went to bed.

The next day, Cain found me as I was packing up to go see about my animals. He said that he wanted to talk to me about the sacrifices. We walked along, and he said how unfair he thought it was that his sacrifice had not pleased God when mine had. All I said was, "Leave me out of it!" Before I knew what was happening, he flew into a rage, snatched the knife out of my sheath, and stabbed me. As I struggled to stay alive, I kept looking into a face that looked a lot like mine—only distorted by rage. I wanted to ask, "What did I do to you?" I never found the strength.

That was the saddest day on earth for my parents because they lost both of their sons! My blood called out to God. My blood's voice put God on notice that something on earth was out of kilter. As my life ebbed away, as my life's blood flowed from my dying body, the God of Life got angry. Cain, who had yielded to anger, was now in deep trouble with an angry God.

God put Cain out of our family that very same day and sent him off alone as a fugitive. For the rage that had taken him over, his punishment was to lose his family. Not only did I die that day but our family life died too! It is horrible what rage will do between family members. My blood continues to cry out, for I was the first of many human beings who have died of family violence!

ISHMAEL & ISAAC

(Genesis 16:1—18:15 and 21:1-21)

Ishmael and Isaac—this is another story in which sibling rivalry plays a role and even causes trouble between parents. Abram's wife, Sarai, was unable to bear him children, so she proposed that Abram use a surrogate mother in the form of her Egyptian slave-girl, Hagar. This is one of the strongest evidences in the Bible that adoption of babies born to surrogate mothers was already being used in ancient Israel.[3]

Ellen Frankel combines scholarship and imagination as she portrays Hagar lamenting because she remained a slave even after conceiving Abram's child. Frankel has Hagar lament: "O women of Israel, pity me! A powerless Egyptian slave, a shadow to Wife Number One, a surrogate womb. My very name suggests 'the wanderer' (hajira), 'the foreigner' (ha-gera), 'the banished one' (ha-gerusha)."[4]

As a slave, Hagar had no power, but once she became pregnant, the tables turned. Since Hagar was able to conceive, it was plain that the infertility was on Sarai's side, not her husband's. The Bible story says that when Hagar saw she had conceived, "she looked with contempt on her mistress." (Gen. 16:4) This was not the result Sarai would have hoped for. She complained to Abram, who told her, "Your slave-girl is in your power; do to her as you please." (Gen. 16:6) Sarai had no mercy. She treated her slave-girl so harshly that Hagar ran away.

An angel of the LORD found Hagar in the wilderness and told her to go back and submit to her mistress, comforting her with a promise: "I will so greatly multiply your offspring that they cannot be counted for multitude....Now you have conceived and shall bear a son; you shall call him Ishmael, for the LORD has given heed to your affliction. He shall be a wild ass of a man, with his hand against everyone, and everyone's hand against him; and he shall live at odds with all his kin." (Gen. 16:10b–12) As the angel predicted, Hagar bore a son and Abram called him Ishmael.

Later, when Abram was 99 years old, the Lord appeared to him and promised to make him the father of many nations, saying he was to change his name to Abraham (meaning "of a great multitude"). His wife was to change her name to Sarah ("princess"). She would bear him a son who would be the father of nations and kings. Far from being overjoyed, Abraham laughed at the idea that Sarah, who was 90 years old, would bear him a son, and he put in a word for his firstborn son, Ishmael. God gently directed Abraham to transfer his hopes to his second son, who was to be named Isaac. God added: "I will establish my covenant with him as an everlasting covenant for his offspring after him. As for Ishmael, I have heard you; I will bless him and make him fruitful and exceedingly numerous; he shall be the father of twelve princes, and I will make him a great nation. But my covenant I will establish with Isaac, whom Sarah shall bear to you at this season next year." (Gen. 17:19b-21)

The next time the Lord appeared to Abraham, Sarah was eavesdropping at the tent door and heard the angel reiterate the promise that she would bear a son. Now Sarah had passed menopause ("it had ceased to be with Sarah after the manner of women," Gen. 18:11b), so she laughed to herself at the idea of two old folks doing what it took to procreate.

Commentary
by Stephanie Biggs-Scribner

Nevertheless, a son was born to Sarah, and Abraham named him Isaac ("laughter"), as God had said.

At Isaac's weaning celebration, something Ishmael did to Isaac made Sarah angry and defensive. She said to Abraham, "Cast out this slave woman with her son; for the son of this slave woman shall not inherit along with my son Isaac." (Gen. 21:10) The Bible story tells us that Abraham was very upset at the thought of losing his first son, so God said to Abraham, "Do not be distressed because of the boy and because of your slave woman; whatever Sarah says to you, do as she tells you, for it is through Isaac that offspring shall be named for you. As for the son of the slave woman, I will make a nation of him also, because he is your offspring." (Gen. 21:12-13) So Abraham gave Hagar some bread and a skin of water and sent her and her child into the wilderness. Here the details of Hagar's story become quite personal and touching.

When the water in the skin was gone, she cast the child under one of the bushes. Then she went and sat down opposite him a good way off, about the distance of a bowshot; for she said, "Do not let me look on the death of the child." And as she sat opposite him, she lifted up her voice and wept. And God heard the voice of the boy; and the angel of God called to Hagar from heaven, and said to her, "What troubles you, Hagar? Do not be afraid; for God has heard the voice of the boy where he is. Come, lift up the boy and hold him fast with your hand, for I will make a great nation of him." Then God opened her eyes and she saw a well of water. She went, and filled the skin with water, and gave the boy a drink. (Gen. 21:15-19)

The Bible tells us that Ishmael survived into adulthood and became a hunter who was skilled with the bow.

This story is difficult for Christian readers. On the one hand, Sarah steps in and prevents a recurrence of the Cain and Abel event. On the other hand, justice in this story seems elusive. What was Ishmael doing that troubled Sarah? Why did Sarah choose such a harsh punishment for Hagar and Ishmael? Why did Abraham agree to send Hagar and Ishmael away? Moreover, why did God tell Abraham to go along with Sarah's desire to banish Ishmael? None of these questions is easily answered, but discussing possible answers may help us grow in theological and textual understanding.

Barely has Isaac come into the story of God's promise to Abraham when the story becomes difficult. It may even take readers several passes through the story before they ask what Ishmael was doing to upset Sarah so greatly. The Hebrew word describing Ishmael's action can mean laugh, play, or tease and has the same root from which Isaac gets his name. It is also the same root describing both Abraham's and Sarah's responses to the news that Sarah would bear a child (Gen 17:17 and 18:10b-12, respectively). Considering the repetition of this root and the response it brings from Sarah, it is an important word. It is characteristic of Hebrew to reuse word roots in multiple contexts. It is likely that in this context what Ishmael is doing is teasing Isaac or mocking him (laughing at him).

Considering the childishness of Ishmael's offense, Sarah's demand for a harsh punishment is difficult to comprehend. It is true that this story does not end with the same tragedy as the story of Cain and Abel, but banishing Hagar and Ishmael into a lonely, dry desert could have ended just as tragically! Renita J. Weems says that "the story of Hagar...is a haunting one. It is a story of exploitation and persecution suffered by an Egyptian slave woman at the hands of her Hebrew mistress." [5] Comparing Abraham's task in this story with his task of sacrificing Isaac in chapter 22, Terence E. Fretheim remarks that the story of Ishmael "is certainly just as difficult and heart-rending." [6] More importantly, he says, "In this story the people of God should recognize and rejoice that God's saving acts are not confined to their own community." [7]

This text reminds us that the world is filled with both physical and spiritual descendants of Ishmael. Nearly one billion Muslims, 85 percent of whom live outside the Middle East, call Abraham father, too. Even more, they are the descendants of God's promise to Ishmael, which remains a contemporary theological reality. How is the other half of Abraham's family going to relate to these brothers and sisters in ways that acknowledge this ongoing work of God? Our words and actions may run so counter to God's activity that the divine will for this people, embodied in the promises, is thereby frustrated and hence less effective than it might otherwise be.[8]

His point is an important one. Christians read this story differently than Muslims. So what differences should Christians know about?

The differences between Christian and Muslim understandings of Isaac and Ishmael are numerous. First of all, in the Islamic holy book, the Koran (or Qur'an), it is understood that Ishmael (Isma'il), not Isaac, was the boy Abraham nearly sacrificed, though he is not named in their text.[9] Second, because of Abraham's willingness to make this sacrifice, he was rewarded with a second son, namely Isaac. Third, Abraham sent Hagar and Ishmael away at Sarah's request even in Islamic tradition, but when they ran out of water, "Hagar...rushed between two hills in anguish."[10] Hagar's "rushing" is connected with the events in Gen. 21:17-21 and is associated with Mecca. Today this running and God's provision of water (believed to have sprung up from beneath the foot of Ishmael) are remembered in an Islamic ritual, part of the hajj (pilgrimage to Mecca), wherein people run between two hills, Safa and Marwah.

In Islamic tradition, Ishmael obviously plays a key role. He is referred to as a prophet. In Genesis 21:16-17, when they have been sent away and have run out of water, both Hagar and Ishmael cry. It is Ishmael's cry to which God responds. The name Ishmael stems from the Hebrew for "whom God hears."

Christian theologian Renita Weems picks up on God's response to Ishmael's cries and offers these prayerful words:

Just as Ishmael must have wept for the senselessness of Hagar, Sarah, and Abraham's ways, maybe it will take our children weeping on our behalf—our children weeping for the sins and prejudices and stubbornness of [us] their mothers and fathers—to convince God to intervene on our behalf. Perhaps as a global community we will be saved—if we are to be saved at all—because of the little children whose innocent tears will prostrate heaven.[11]

The story about God's response to a boy's tears stirs us even after thousands of years. Part of our response to the way this story touches us is to wonder why Abraham agreed to Sarah's demand that Hagar and Ishmael be sent away into the desert. Were the parental responses to sibling rivalry appropriate?

Answering the question is simple in Abraham's case. He agrees to part with his son because God says he must. (Gen. 21:12) But why does this story, deemed holy by so many people, portray God as counseling Abraham to let Sarah send Hagar and Ishmael away? Could it be that by allowing them to be sent away, God was able to perform yet another miracle in making a nation of Ishmael? (Gen. 21:13)

Abraham's story in the Hebrew Bible is fragmented, appearing like a broken vase pieced together for coherence. This trait is common to ancient stories and has led numerous scholars to conclude that they were made up of multiple traditions. Taking any version of the story, such as the one we have before us today, labeling it as the authoritative standard, and insisting that such a standard be taken in only one way obscures the history behind the assembling of the text. Moreover, it stalls readers from asking what may be beneficial questions about the story. The result of reading ancient stories like these without considering other versions may be that we miss out on incredible new possibilities. Might Abraham be the father of twice as many multitudes as most Christians suspect? What if the mothers of his current children sought ways to coexist respectfully? What if Abraham's children learned to get along?

LETTERS ON THE STORY OF ISHMAEL AND ISAAC

by Stephanie and Maggie Biggs-Scribner

Dear Maggie,

Even though I already know you well since I am your mother, I feel like I'm getting know you even better by writing these letters! I'm happy that we're doing this!

I know you remember the stories of Abraham and Sarah. They are famous ancestors of our Jewish friends, and ancestors of Jesus, too. This story happens before their names are even Abraham and Sarah. In this story, they are first called Abram and Sarai, and the story is about them trying to have a baby. They must have tried without success for a long time, because when our story begins, they are very old. They even consider Sarai too old to have a baby, although Abram isn't too old to become a daddy, because it doesn't work the same way for men as it does for women.

Since they think Sarai is too old to have a baby, they decide that Abram should father a child by someone else and Sarai should adopt it. Sarai chooses her slave, Hagar, to be the mother she will adopt from. When the baby is born, it's a boy and his name is Ishmael. His name means "the one God hears." Isn't that beautiful? His name ends up being a great blessing for him and even for people alive today! Here's how.

Even though Abram and Sarai technically have a baby, Ishmael, God still promises Abram that Sarai will get to be pregnant and have a baby from her own body. Sarai is very old, so when she overhears it, she laughs. Even so, a baby is finally born, and he is named Isaac (a name that comes from the word "to laugh"). Now, even his parents have new names, Abraham and Sarah.

It's kind of weird, though. They name Isaac a name associated with laughing, but when Sarah sees Ishmael teasing (or "laughing at") Isaac, she sends Ishmael and Hagar, his birth mother, away into the desert. Abraham is very upset to lose his first son, but just think of poor Ishmael and Hagar—how they suffer in the heat! They almost die without water to drink! Ishmael and Hagar cry. Genesis says that God hears Ishmael cry and shows them water. God even promises that Ishmael will live and become an entire nation of people!

I'm glad that in the story, nothing bad happens to Ishmael and Hagar. But I think it's scary to imagine a dad sending his kid and the kid's mom away with barely any food. I know that faith is an important thing, but kindness and compassion are important too.

Do you know which people consider themselves descendants of Ishmael? It is people of the Islamic faith. Your Muslim friends probably think of Ishmael as their fore-father! When God hears someone crying, God responds in a big way, huh? Have you ever wished for God to hear you when you cried? I sure have.

Love, Mom

Dear Mom,

I wish God would hear me when I'm trapped in a sticky situation and all I can do is watch my life become a puzzle with about 5,000 pieces. That's the time I need God most! A couple of years ago when I was eight, I was thinking about this story and said to myself, "Wow, Sarai was so eager to have a kid she didn't care if it was completely hers or not!"

In a way, I think Abraham was desperate too. He wanted a holy child, and then once he got one he wanted another one. I guess the word I'm looking for isn't desperate, it's greedy. I'm glad he cared about both of them, though. Most of my friends don't live with their dad, and some don't live with their parents at all. They live with grandparents, or godmothers, or godfathers, so it's nice that Abraham was unhappy when Ishmael had to go away.

Love,
Maggie

A DIFFERENT VIEW: ISHMAEL *by Linda H. Hollies*

I was born to a wealthy man and a slave woman. Talk about confusion—I know what it means. I was born out of a relationship arranged by the woman who owned my mother and by the woman's husband, Abram. Talk about tension—I know how it feels. My little brother, Isaac, was born when I was 13. Sometimes I enjoyed having him around; at other times I was annoyed by the special treatment he seemed to get. Talk about feeling conflicted. I was the firstborn son and should have received most of my father's wealth. Talk about feeling denied, abandoned, and rejected when my mother and I were sent away from our home to die in the desert!

My mother, Hagar, was an Egyptian slave in the family of Abram and Sarai, the leaders of God's chosen people. She was sort of a ladies' maid who waited upon the mistress in a home of great wealth. My mother was a beautiful woman who worked diligently and always knew that her place was to be an obedient slave.

The Most High God of Abram had sent him away from his homeland on a lengthy and strange journey, promising him so many children that they would be as hard to number as the grains of sand or even as the stars in the sky. Abram and Sarai, along with Abram's father and his nephew, Lot, walked away from all that was familiar and comfortable to begin a new nation that would be called the people of God. Somewhere along the line, Abram began to accumulate great wealth. In those days, wealth included slaves who did the physical work.

As the couple aged and had no child, both of them began to worry about God's promise that had not been fulfilled. It was during this time, when my father was close to 90 years old, that Sarai came up with the plan. To help make God's promise come true, she would ask Abram to use my mother, Hagar, to have a baby.

Slavery is so complex. Slavery makes people into things. Slavery means that someone is the owner and someone else is owned. My mother "belonged" to Abram and Sarai. There were no questions asked. There has always been this custom of people thinking that they "own" other human beings. My mother knew her place as a slave. And Sarai knew that any child born of Abram and her slave would become her property. This is the thought Sarai had when I was conceived.

It might sound funny, but I just wanted to be born. God had chosen me to come to earth as the child of a man from whom I, as the oldest son, would inherit great wealth. This was the culture of the nation that was being formed, and it sounded like a good plan to me. My father had absolute power as head of the nation and of his family, but when they could not get pregnant, he allowed his wife to dictate what sounded like a good idea to him. He wasn't duped. He was willing to go along to have God's promise fulfilled.

I am a child of promise and possibility and potential. I was not a mistake. I was planned, and I was wanted by all three individuals who were involved. My mother felt that being pregnant when Sarai could not get pregnant would give her more significance in the household. Sarai, knowing that I would "belong" to her and to Abram, felt that she would be known no longer as a "barren" woman. And my father, Abram, called "the father of the nation," felt that he would be looked upon as a potent man.

It sounded like everyone would be happy if my mother, Hagar, got pregnant. But life is never without complications. In my family, my mother's pregnancy brought about major problems, for my mother began to feel very important when she got pregnant. Sarai had never imagined that a slave woman could have feelings of self-esteem, but something within my mother gave her a feeling that she was bringing a special child into the world. She did not originally believe in Abram's God, but the god of the master and mistress became the god of their slaves too. So my mother became a believer and knew that Abram was someone important to God! Having Abram's child, therefore, made her important too. I surely felt that she was important!

Mrs. Abram got fighting mad at my mother's attitude. To make matters worse, she put all the blame on my dad! She said that God had to decide who was right in the plan that she had concocted in the first place. Go figure! Sarai became so mean and abusive toward my mother, Hagar, that she ran away! Now, I had not been born yet, but I was there in Hagar's womb.

When my mother had walked a good way into the wilderness, she sat beside a spring of water and God sent an angel to see about us. I told you I was special to God! The angel asked Mom, "What are you doing here?" When my mother said that we were running away, the angel said to her: "Go back to your mistress. Put up with her abuse. I'm going to give you a big family, children past counting." I was right there and I heard the entire conversation!

Can you imagine—this was the very same promise that God had given to my father years before? Can you believe that my mother, a foreigner and a slave, was given a promise by the Creator of the world? Because my mother patiently obeyed the orders of Mrs. Abram, she was pulled into the covenant that God made with the head of a new nation. Talk about a big promotion! The angel even told my mother to name me Ishmael, which means "the one God hears."

The angel told my mother just how I would act when I grew up. "He'll be a bucking bronco of a man, a real rebel, fighting and being fought, always stirring up trouble, always at odds with his family." (Genesis 16:12, rephrased.) I didn't plan to have sibling rivalry. It grew out of my situation, for Abram and Sarai didn't treat my mother as they should have. My mother, as a stranger in the land, was entitled to be treated with respect, dignity, and hospitality. These are the hallmarks of God's chosen people.

I was 14, well established as the firstborn son, when my little brother was born. Dad was now called Abraham, and his wife's name was Sarah. All the males in our community had been circumcised as the new symbol of being God's chosen people. Dad and I were circumcised on the same day. It was a bonding ritual, for other nations did not cut the foreskins off their boys.

Now Mrs. Abraham had her own baby and they named him Isaac, which means "laughter." I was excited about becoming a big brother. I was waiting to teach him all the things I had learned. As a male, I stayed outside among the other men and didn't have much of a relationship with Mrs. Abraham. However, my mother continued in her role as a lady-in-waiting. She'd had a son by a great man, but she remained a slave.

I'll never forget the day we left home, for it was at Isaac's weaning party that Mrs. Abraham saw me poking fun at my new little brother. She threw a fit, and she demanded that my father put us out! "Get rid of this slave woman and her son. No child of this slave is going to share the inheritance with my son Isaac!" And God told my father to go along with her madness!

Where were we to go? How were we to survive? How were we to carry our few belongings without mules, camels, or wagons? Both my mother and I were feeling loss. We couldn't believe our ears. We had survived over 14 years of Sarah's strange behaviors and had never seen this day coming! Suddenly we were homeless. We were to become wanderers. We were thrown out like trash. We had no place to belong.

I could see the glee on Mrs. Abraham's face when my father said we had to leave. My father had a look of pain and tears in his eyes, yet he didn't stand up for his right to keep us. Early the next morning, he got us up, gave us some bread and a canteen of water, and sent us on our way to only God knew where. Abraham told my mother not to worry! He reminded her that God had promised to develop a great nation out of me because I was his flesh and blood too. But who cared about that? I didn't want to leave the only home I'd ever known! I had a new little brother to raise, to teach, and to love!

It was certainly a gloomy day in our life. We faced an uncertain future. We had no road map into the next day. We were without a backup plan or reserve provisions. Yet my mother faced straight ahead. You would never know that she had spent her life as a slave. I tell you, Hagar dared me to look back with longing. She told me that she had better not see a tear or hear a sniffle. It was the look of determination on my mother's face that said to me, "Move one foot ahead of the other. All is well!"

THE YOUNG JOSEPH

(Genesis 30:22—33:20 and 37:1-36)

This story involves parental favoritism that leads to sibling rivalry. The story of Joseph is full of so much intrigue that it has inspired plays, movies, and stories dubbing him the "King of Dreams" and calling the special coat made by his father, the "Amazing Technicolor Dreamcoat."[12]

Most of the verses declared above as involving Joseph (Gen. 30:22—33:20) do not often mention Joseph in a direct way. Rachel, his mother, who has had difficulty getting pregnant, finally conceives and bears Joseph. (Gen. 30:22-24)[13] The story credits Rachel's successful conception and delivery to God: "Then God remembered Rachel, and God heeded her and opened her womb. She conceived and bore a son, and said, 'God has taken away my reproach.'" (Gen. 30:22-23) She names her son Joseph because God "added" a son into her life and she wishes for more. (Gen. 30:24) The name Joseph ("he shall add") typifies the Hebrew wordplays used in naming.[14]

During the time when Jacob fathers his first 10 sons, he, his wives, and their children live with Laban, the father of Jacob's wives Leah and Rachel. Once Joseph, his first child by Rachel, is born, Jacob begins requesting Laban to allow him, his wives, and their children to leave. (Gen. 30:25-26) Laban does not immediately agree, but initiates discussion of the terms under which Jacob will be allowed to take his family and go. (Gen. 30:27-34) Implementing the terms of this agreement causes

Commentary
by Stephanie Biggs-Scribner

strife between Jacob and Laban's sons, drawing out the time of Jacob's family's departure.

Similarly, the story of how Jacob and his family actually arrive at their new home and get reacquainted with Jacob's extended family is a lengthy one. In fact, it is not until Genesis 37 that the story turns to focus on the story of sibling rivalry between Joseph and his brothers. When Joseph is 17 years old, he brings Jacob "a bad report" about four of his half-brothers. (Gen. 37:2) This sets the stage for a story of terrible revenge. Verse 3 elaborates: "Now Israel loved Joseph more than any other of his children, because he was the son of his old age; and he had made him a long robe with sleeves." The brothers respond badly to this favoritism. (Gen. 37:4) To make matters worse, Joseph dreams that objects representing his family will bow to an object that represents him—and he tactlessly tells his family about these dreams! (Gen. 37:5-11)

Joseph's dreams become a source of enmity between him and his brothers. His dreams are even declared to be the reason for Joseph's being sent into Egypt. However, Egypt is not the first choice of destinations his brothers have in mind for him. When Joseph's brothers are caring for the flock, Jacob (whom God has now renamed Israel) sends Joseph to bring a report on their well-being. (Gen. 37:13-14) The brothers see him coming and, according to the story, plan to kill him to "see what will become of his dreams." (Gen. 37:20) His oldest brother, Reuben (Leah and Jacob's firstborn), steps in and saves his life. (Gen. 37:21-22) Joseph is thrown into a pit, and his special coat, a symbol of his father's favoritism, is taken from him. (Gen.

37:23-24) Reuben plans to rescue him later. Meanwhile, the other brothers sit down to lunch. Reuben is not present when a caravan going to Egypt passes by. Verses 25-28 say the travelers are Ishmaelite traders taking gum, balm, and resin to Egypt.

Joseph's brother Judah sees the caravan as an opportunity to stop a murder from taking place. The text is not clear about whether Judah's thought for Joseph's life is guided more strongly by compassion ("[Let us] not lay our hands on him, for he is our brother, our own flesh") or by greed ("What profit is it if we kill our brother and conceal his blood? Come, let us sell him to the Ishmaelites"). The brothers agree to sell Joseph to the travelers, and they send his special coat back to their father dipped in goat's blood to prove that a wild animal attacked him. Without remorse, they leave Jacob to mourn Joseph's death. At this point, we as readers do not yet know the full extent of what becomes of Joseph. But we do see that the terrible anger driving Joseph's brothers might have been averted if Israel had tried to treat all his children equally.

LETTERS ON THE YOUNG JOSEPH
by Stephanie and Maggie Biggs-Scribner

Dear Maggie,

Now on to our next story, Joseph. You are already familiar with this story because of the musical we have about it. You remember that, when Joseph is a teenager, his older brothers get jealous because of the special coat their dad makes for him and mad because of the dreams he brags about to them, so they plan to kill him. Thank goodness, one brother, Reuben, gets the other brothers to throw Joseph into a pit instead of killing him. Reuben plans to come back and rescue him later. But while he's away, the others sell Joseph to some travelers going to Egypt. They tell their dad that Joseph is dead. Remember that song they sing in our movie—about how sad they are that "poor Joseph" is dead?

The travelers take Joseph to Egypt, where he lives for many years. Through his gift of interpreting dreams, Joseph winds up working for Pharaoh and storing up food to last Egypt through a famine. The famine gets so bad that his family runs out of food and has to go to Egypt to keep from starving. When Joseph's brothers get to Egypt to buy some food for their father, Joseph tells them that even though they tried to be mean to him, God made it all work together for good, since now he can save their lives. Do you think it must have been hard for Joseph to forgive them?

Love, Mom

23

Dear Mom,

Yes, it must have been hard for Joseph to forgive them, but it had been a long time so it might have been easier than it looked. I'm just glad everything turned out all right! I wish everything would always turn out well. I think it was odd that all the brothers wanted to kill him and then they decided to sell him. I'm not all that sure about what I would do if I had a brother that my father favored. I do remember the movie you're talking about, and I remember the song too. I think that movie is funny and I enjoyed watching it. My favorite part in the song is "Joseph, the things that you stood ferr, lahke truth 'n love, neverr die!"

Love, Maggie

A DIFFERENT VIEW OF THE YOUNG JOSEPH: ALWAYS AN OUTSIDER *by Linda H. Hollies*

I seem to have inherited the quality of always being the outsider from both sides of my family.

My father's name is now Israel, which means "soldier of God," but he was born and named Jacob ("supplanter"). He stole the birthright from his older twin, Esau, and had to run away from home to live. He was taken in by his mother's brother, Laban, but was treated like an outsider. Laban tricked him into tending flocks for 14 years in order to marry my mother.

My mother's name is Rachel, and my father loved her very deeply. Laban said that if Jacob would work for seven years, he would win the right to marry her. But she was younger than her sister, Leah, and because Laban wanted his older daughter to marry first, Leah was slipped into the marriage tent on the night of the wedding. My mother wept all night long, knowing that now she was the outsider. Laban would make Jacob work another seven years before she could be his wife. It was years after that before she had a child.

I was not born until both of my parents were old, so my father was very attached to me as a child of his old age. When my mother died giving birth to my little brother, Benjamin, all of the love that my father had for my mother was transferred to me. I did not choose to be my father's favorite, but I needed his love so I stayed as close to him as possible.

All my older brothers had a mother and they had each other, plus they had my father. I was the outsider. This did not make me feel special. I tried hard to be included in the closeness of my other brothers, but it never worked. They thought I was spoiled. They sensed that I was our father's favorite.

One year, our father made me a special long-sleeved coat of many different colors. That made my brothers hate me even more.

Being an outsider makes you withdraw into yourself. Most fathers are not emotional, sharing, and talkative people. I knew my father's love, but I didn't know my father's mind or thinking. I knew that my father was a great man with much influence because of God. I also knew that God had great expectations of our family. So, like my father, I began to pray and to seek God for myself. Then God began to speak to me in dreams.

I didn't know what the dreams meant. They were confusing. For example, in one dream we were all in the field binding sheaves. Suddenly, my sheaf stood upright and all my brothers' sheaves bowed down before it. That made no sense. I was not the favored son according to our traditions. Reuben was the oldest son. He was the one I looked up to, for he was tall and strong and would be in charge when my father died. However, my dreams were not telling me that Reuben was going to be the leader. I needed some help with figuring out what these dreams meant, so I thought I might share them with my big brothers.

One day Father sent me out in the fields to check on my brothers and take them some provisions. I thought this would be a good chance to tell them about my dreams. When I described my dreams to my brothers, they got fighting mad. They called me all kinds of names. They didn't help me work out my dreams' meaning. Instead they drove me away and I ran home. When they returned from the fields, they told father that I was crazy, and my father began to wonder about me. I remained silent, but the dreams did not cease.

One night while they were home, I dreamed that the sun, moon, and eleven stars were bowing down before me. The next day I told the dream to my whole family. Boy, was I dumb! Even my father went into a rage. I was not asking for these dreams. It was not my fault that God was sending me messages in my dreams. I became still more of an outsider. I even began to feel distant from my father. My heart was heavy, for I wanted—I *needed*—to know where I belonged.

After that horrible incident with my father and my brothers, I became silent and more withdrawn. Still the dreams did not stop, and I knew that God had a divine purpose for my life. I just didn't understand what all of this would mean.

Again, my father sent me out on a mission to the fields where my brothers were. As soon as my brothers saw me coming, I could see them pointing and laughing. I could guess that they were mocking me and calling me names like "the Dreamer," but I never would have guessed there was a plan among my own flesh and blood to kill me! Now I learned they hated me enough to have planned to murder me! My brother Reuben called a halt to the murder, but the others ripped my special coat off me and threw me into a pit. There was no water down there and it was dark. I was really scared, so I prayed a lot. After a while they pulled me out, but it was only to sell me to a group of strangers! Reuben wasn't there to save me again.

Not one of my other older brothers showed any remorse. Instead, they plotted to tell my father that I had been killed by a wild animal. They covered my special coat with blood as a proof of my death.

Their hatred sears my mind. God's failure to make the messages of the dreams come true crushes my heart. God has disappeared. I'm on my way to a foreign land where no one even knows my name! How am I to remain faithful to a God who allows such things to happen? If there is a reason for everything I'm going through, I can't see it yet.

THE CANAANITE WOMAN'S DAUGHTER

(Matthew 15:21-28; Mark 7:24-30)

In this account, a girl is the subject of the story but she is not present. While the child's well-being hangs in the balance, adults argue about seemingly unrelated issues.

Matthew uses the generic term *Canaanite* for this woman's origin, but Mark is very specific: she is a Syrophoenician (living in the coastal part of Syria). Jesus has traveled to Tyre and does not want to be noticed by people. The version in Matthew says:

> *Jesus left that place and went away to the district of Tyre and Sidon. Just then a Canaanite woman from that region came out and started shouting, "Have mercy on me, Lord, Son of David; my daughter is tormented by a demon." But he did not answer her at all. And his disciples came and urged him, saying, "Send her away, for she keeps shouting after us." He answered, "I was sent only to the lost sheep of the house of Israel." But she came and knelt before him, saying, "Lord, help me." He answered, "It is not fair to take the children's food and throw it to the dogs." She said, "Yes, Lord, yet even the dogs eat the crumbs that fall from their masters' table." Then Jesus answered her, "Woman, great is your faith! Let it be done for you as you wish." And her daughter was healed instantly. (Matt. 15:21-28)*

Just one of the difficulties this story presents to readers today is the dramatic portrayal of the child's illness. What are we to make of the "demon" troubling the child? In the time of Jesus, demons were regarded as part of the "spirit world," which was considered as "real" as the physical world of touch, taste, and smell. Demons were thought of as beings that inhabited the realm between the gods and the world of mortals. At times, demons supposedly took possession of the bodies of mortals, most often bringing about manic or violent behavior. If a person was acting psychotic, the person was branded as demon-possessed. It was believed that expulsion of the demon would bring about restoration of health and sanity. According to Arndt and Gingrich, this was a common worldview at the time of Jesus and his disciples.[15]

There are several other New Testament stories in which Jesus and his followers deal with possessed individuals, including Matthew 7:22-23, Matthew 8:28-34, Mark 5:1-20, Mark 16:17, and Luke 9:49-50. The story in Mark 5 (and Matthew 8)—telling how Jesus makes a wild man's demons enter a herd of swine, which then goes dashing madly down a slope into the Sea of Galilee—gives the most graphic illustration of the demon-possessed state.

Nowadays, we have more academic-sounding names, such as schizophrenia, for "possessed" behavior, but perhaps our current clinical terms will be shown to be as inexact as "demon possession" when such illnesses are better understood. One certainty about the Syrophoenician woman is that she felt her child was out of control. Most probably the child was in early adolescence when mental illnesses began to manifest themselves in ways that could not be ignored.

Mark 7:25 describes the Syrophoenician woman's little daughter as suffering from an "unclean spirit." This term comes from the Greek words *pneuma akatharton* (while "demon," as in Matthew 15 above, comes from *daemon*). The root

Commentary
by Stephanie Biggs-Scribner

pneuma, which is where the word *pneumonia* comes from, has to do with breathing and lungs. One of its meanings is "spirit." A similar word in Hebrew is *ruah* (breath, wind), which is also used to mean spirit. Both Matthew and Mark imply that this child with an illness affecting her spirit is in need of an exorcism. Whatever the nature of her problem, the child has been brought to Jesus for healing. But Jesus (the miracle worker of Mark 5) says, "It is not fair to take the children's food and throw it to the dogs." Matthew and Mark are unanimous on this wording.

When faced with the difficulty of having an ill child, a mother sought help. Of all things to be faced with, now she is in the position of having to convince an apparently unwilling Jesus to help! It is not difficult to imagine the bruised ego or anger that might have been caused by a comment like his. But the story does not describe the mother as being stalled by Jesus' response. Rather, she accepts being classed as a dog and uses her wits to make a quick comeback: "Yes, Lord, yet even the dogs eat the crumbs that fall from their masters' table." (Matt. 15:27)

It is unfortunate that in order to have her daughter cared for, the woman in this story must resort to belittling herself. We may be left wondering for years to come why the early Christian community found such a story worthy of canonization (the process through which texts became officially accepted as part of the Christian Testament). A mother putting her child's needs above her own is not a surprising picture, but Jesus' response is puzzling.

Another aspect of this story needs to be considered carefully—its international implications. Obviously the woman's Gentile lineage plays a crucial role. We must consider the implication of this story in its original context, and we must also consider the text's subsequent interpretation through the ages. Musa Dube relates the story to today's continuing colonial attitudes and realities. The Gentile mother represents "foreigners who appear in stories they did not write."[16] For the Jews of Jesus' own time, the story shows an authoritative Jewish leader prevailing over a group of outsiders—Gentiles. For Musa Dube, the story "constructs a politically unsubversive Jesus and encourages travel to distant and inhabited lands."[17]

In envisioning the mission to the nations, Matthew's model embodies imperialistic values and strategies. It does not seek relationships of liberating interdependence between nations, cultures, and genders. Rather, it upholds the superiority of some races and advocates the subjugation of differences by relegating other races to inferiority.[18]

When reading stories like that of the Gentile mother, we are made aware of how painful Bible stories can become when they are used without an awareness of or concern for our neighbors. Being responsible readers requires growing in sensitivity. Readers cannot always be aware of angles by which various stories have been used for harm. Neither can readers simply abolish every story that has ever been used harmfully. But readers can remain open to the understandings of other readers, and they can use dialogue with other kinds of readers to create and sustain healthy interpretations of stories like this one. What if the woman had simply asked Jesus, "What makes you think I'm as low as a dog?" Would Jesus have said, "Because you don't have a quick wit and a clever answer, I won't heal your daughter"?

LETTERS ON THE CANAANITE WOMAN'S DAUGHTER

by Stephanie and Maggie Biggs-Scribner

Dear Maggie,

You might find the next story interesting. It's about a lady who needs her daughter healed. The lady is not Jewish like Jesus. She shouts to Jesus to have mercy on her daughter, who she says is tormented by an unclean spirit. But Jesus doesn't even answer her! She doesn't give up though. She pleads until finally the disciples ask Jesus to get rid of her. Instead, Jesus does something odd. He says that he was sent only to the "lost sheep" of Israel. And still the mother doesn't give up! She gets on her knees and says, "Lord, help me." Now Jesus says something amazing to her. See what you think about it. He says, "It is not fair to take the children's food and throw it to the dogs." She answers that even the dogs eat the crumbs from under the master's table. So Jesus says that her faith is huge and her request has been granted. Her daughter is healed instantly!

Maggie, this story takes place on the edges of Israel, right where some Canaanites lived who had inhabited the "Promised Land" before the Jews took it. If you remember your dad and me talking about how hard it was for the Native Americans when our ancestors moved in and started making the United States, then you can understand a little bit of what is going on in this New Testament story. The Gentile lady was part of the group that had been pushed out of their native land, and she wanted her daughter healed by a man who belonged to the group that had pushed them out. So when she has the courage to go up to him and beg for her daughter to be healed, her faith is teaching us a lesson: we should always be ready for God to surprise us from unexpected people and places. Has God ever surprised you?

Love,
Mom

Dear Mom,

I really can't answer your question about being surprised by God, because I'm not sure when God is the one I'm talking with and when it's not. But if I did know, I would probably be surprised a lot, because a lot of kooky stuff happens to me, and it's so weird I don't think I can explain it in any other way that makes sense. I don't like the fact that Jesus basically just called her a dog. But I do like the fact that because she was stubborn she got her way. I don't think it was right to test her like that. It was a mean thing to do. I can relate to her a little bit. It's like when you know someone is wrong about something and you try to tell them what's correct, but they won't listen and you get stubborn and rude because you're trying to show them, but they won't let you. I'm glad she doesn't give up.

Love, Maggie

A DIFFERENT VIEW OF THE CANAANITE WOMAN'S DAUGHTER: THE IDENTIFIED PATIENT *by Linda H. Hollies*

In every family there is one person who is always blamed for the craziness that is within the family. This person, sometimes called the "identified patient," is only acting out the symptoms of the entire family. In my family, I get a lot of blame.

My story is now famous, but my name is never mentioned. Yet my mother thought long and hard about what my name was to be. It's not unusual in the telling of stories about young girls like me for us to be unnamed, but the fact that my name is not mentioned does make me feel invisible and very insignificant. I have a name. I have a distinct personality. And I am not crazy!

People tend to forget that when the Jews moved into "their" Promised Land, we Canaanites who had lived there for generations were displaced! The very houses that my ancestors had built were taken from them. The very vineyards, gardens, and wells that my ancestors had dug became the "property" of people who came in and took over. We Canaanites were homeless in the land of our birth. We were "the others" in the very place where our ancestors had lived. When people tell our story they forget this minor fact.

Homelessness tends to makes you act crazy! My mother tried her best to make life "normal" for our family. But how can you be "normal" living without a place to call home? How can you be "normal" when you are treated as a heathen and thought to be beneath another group?

Our lives consisted of searching and begging and seeking for safe places to live. Our days were spent without a place to call home, without enough to eat, and without any protection from constant slights and insults. We were no longer the proud and powerful people that we had been before the invaders came. We had become "the minority," as the newcomers multiplied and took over. The more they made themselves at home, the more we were pushed to the edges out of their sight. It wasn't right. It wasn't fair. It made me angry. I began to hate the people who took over and I started to rebel against them!

My father had disappeared, along with many other proud men who could not live with being treated as if they were invisible. That included my uncles and male cousins, too. We women and girls were left by ourselves, trying to keep a settlement going along the walls of a town in the district of Tyre and Sidon near the border with Judea.

I got so hungry that I learned how to steal. I went to the fields and acted like I was the little girl of one of the workers. When no one was looking, I took food for my mother and me. My mother was afraid that I was going to be caught and killed for stealing. But somebody had to act.

Whenever a girl breaks the rules—no matter how unfair they are—she's labeled "crazy." If our life had been "normal," I might have been a nice little girl. Instead, I was a ringleader among the other girls. Some of them began to follow me on my food raids, and our mothers got even more frightened. My mother said that she was going to

go and get me some help. All I wanted my mother to do was to help me make things better!

Mother went straight over to a "First Church of Jesus" meeting. Of course she was very nervous, for the church members did not like those they called "foreigners" and "Gentiles." My mother knew that it was against their rules for a woman to be in the same room with a male teacher, but she was determined that I would come back to my "right mind," as she called it. What is the right mind for someone who is thought to be inferior in every way?

We were all depressed. Depression is a slow, dull anger at something you can't fix. My mother broke into this religious meeting and begged the leader, Jesus, for help. "Son of David," she cried, "have mercy on me. My daughter is afflicted by an evil spirit." I became the "identified patient" for our entire nation! In reality, we were all sick in spirit.

Jesus' disciples urged him to send my mother away. It was then that Jesus compared us to dogs since we weren't members of the First Church. Jesus said it wouldn't be fair for him "to take the children's food and throw it to the dogs."

My mother heard the insult but used the language of the powerless. She said, "Yet even the dogs eat the crumbs that fall from their master's table."

Jesus liked the quick wit of her answer. She showed him that faith in God wasn't limited to his group. So he granted her plea. She ran all the way home to hug me and tell me the story. "This Jesus is a Jew and a healer," she said. "He listened to me! Look at you! You're healed! You have hope in your eyes again."

"All of a sudden, the hate just left me," I told her. "I'll always fight for what's fair and right, but I don't feel hopeless anymore."

My mother's great, courageous faith gave even Jesus an awakening. After meeting her, he turned around his whole agenda of salvation. Instead of limiting himself to the Jews, he would offer his gifts and God's grace to everyone! Now not just one patient but the whole world can be healed! That is good news indeed!

Part 2

CHILDREN
UNDER THREAT

THE BABY MOSES

(Exodus 2:1-10)

Previous stories in Genesis declared that the Children of Israel (Jacob and his offspring) went to Egypt in order to survive a famine. (Gen. 46) According to the continuation of these stories in Exodus, the Hebrews did more than survive the famine; they flourished. (Ex. 1:7) In time, a new Pharaoh came to rule over Egypt, one who did not know Joseph. The new Pharaoh did not have the same generous attitude as the first Pharaoh. He feared that the Hebrews were becoming a threat to national security, so he set them to work doing hard labor on his building projects. (Ex. 1:9-11)

When even that did not stop the Hebrews from multiplying numerously, the Pharaoh ordered two Hebrew midwives, Shiphrah and Puah, to kill all the baby boys born to Hebrew women. (Ex. 1:15-16) The midwives pretended that they were not speedy enough to intercept Hebrew babies at birth, saying that the Hebrew women were so hardy that they gave birth before the midwives could get there. Because the midwives' wily tactics foiled the plans of the Pharaoh to cut back on population growth among the Hebrews, he commanded all of his people: "Every boy that is born to the Hebrews you shall throw into the Nile." (Ex. 1:22a) Into this story of cultural mayhem, Moses, a man of Levite lineage, was born.

Now a man from the house of Levi went and married a Levite woman. The woman conceived and bore a son; and when she saw that he was a fine baby, she hid him three months. When she could hide him no longer she got a papyrus basket for him, and plastered it with bitumen and pitch; she put the child in it and placed it among the reeds on the bank of the river. His sister stood at a distance, to see what would happen to him. The daughter of Pharaoh came down to bathe at the river, while her attendants walked beside the river. She saw the basket among the reeds and sent her maid to bring it. When she opened it, she saw the child. He was crying, and she took pity on him, "This must be one of the Hebrews' children," she said. Then his sister said to Pharaoh's daughter, "Shall I go and get you a nurse from the Hebrew women to nurse the child for you?" Pharaoh's daughter said to her, "Yes." So the girl went and called the child's mother. Pharaoh's daughter said to her, "Take this child and nurse it for me, and I will give you your wages." So the woman took the child and nursed it. When the child grew up, she brought him to Pharaoh's daughter, and she took him as her son. She named him Moses, "because," she said, "I drew him out of the water." (Ex. 2:1-10)

Commentary
by Stephanie Biggs-Scribner

The story of Moses' birth is filled with ironies and surprising turns of events. For one thing, the very source of the threat to Moses' life ends up being the source of his salvation: not just Egypt itself in general but, more specifically, an Egyptian river. For another, this man who comes to be a heroic leader of the Hebrews is not named by his Hebrew mother but by an Egyptian woman. Moreover, this story is tied to the stories in Genesis by more than just the Joseph narrative explaining how the children of Israel came to be in Egypt. (Gen. 46 and 47) It is also tied to the Genesis stories by the basket that saves Moses. The basket into which his mother puts him is literally an "ark" in Hebrew, just as was used in the Noah story to save the lives of his family and all humanity.

Another surprising piece of this story is the lack of names in it. What was Moses' mother's name? What was his father's? Was the sister who stood guard at the river in Exodus 2:4 the prophet Miriam of Exodus 15:20? What was the name of Pharaoh's daughter? Yet even without this information, the story functions in its own way.

About the story of Moses' birth, Walter Brueggemann declares that it "is not fundamentally interested in the person of Moses." Rather than relate much about Moses' young life, the story "moves quickly...to the violent urgency of adulthood."[19] In other words, the namelessness in this story may function to direct readers to an important point within it—that the rescue of Moses "anticipates a larger rescue to be wrought through the power of Moses."[20] This story is not focusing on Moses per se but is harking back to the very early Genesis story of Noah and the salvation of humanity. Moreover, when Moses' mother sees that he is a "fine" baby, the word she uses to describe him matches exactly with the word used to describe God's creation in Genesis 1:1-4 (translated there as "good"). The intricacies in Moses' birth story lead us to understand that the story is about the creation of the Hebrew people. When Moses' mother saved his life by sending him away floating in an "ark" and then nursed him as the child of an Egyptian woman, she saved an entire nation of people who were yet to be born.

LETTERS ON THE BABY MOSES
by Stephanie and Maggie Biggs-Scribner

Dear Maggie,

You know that protecting the child is an important concern for any parent. In your class at school you are studying child labor, so you also know that sometimes the community around the child does not protect the child as it should. It's terrible when a community does not protect a child. It has always been a problem, not just nowadays. So it makes sense that there's a story about it in the Bible.

Remember the story of baby Moses in Egypt being put into a basket and pushed out into a river where the daughter of the Pharaoh found him and saved him? That's the story I want to share with you first. It's a beautifully written story with lots of poetic details.

First let me remind you why the mom put Moses into a basket that floated on the river. The ruler of Egypt, the Pharaoh, had ordered that all the baby boys of the Hebrew people were to be killed! Isn't that terrible? The story in Exodus explains that the Hebrews were getting so numerous that the Pharaoh was afraid of them. Maybe he thought they might try to take over. The story as it's found in Exodus 2 doesn't tell us the Pharaoh's name. It doesn't tell us the name of Moses' mom or dad either. It seems weird for a story to skip over such important things, but some people think the story does it in order to focus on a bigger point: the story of the Hebrew people.

See, to understand the "bigger point" of the story, we have to remember the story about Joseph and his jealous brothers. Joseph's brothers sell him to some passing traders in a caravan going down to Egypt. Through his ability to interpret dreams, Joseph becomes the Pharaoh's second-in-command. He helps save Egypt from starvation by arranging to store up food during seven years of good harvest. When a drought comes, Egypt is the only land in the region where there is any food. Joseph's brothers and his father all wind up going down to Egypt so they won't starve. Remember they find Joseph there?

Well, much later all the Hebrews live in Egypt, but a different Pharaoh is in charge. He makes the people work like slaves. It is so long after Joseph's day that the new Pharaoh doesn't even care that Joseph helped Egypt get through a famine. By the time the Moses story starts, there are so many Hebrews in Egypt that the new Pharaoh is worried. He wants to kill all the baby boys to keep the population from growing. But a woman from the tribe of Levi has a fine baby boy and does not want to him to die. She hides him for three months. When she can't hide him anymore, she builds an "ark" to put him in and floats the ark among the reeds in the river where the Pharaoh's daughter will find it.

The Pharaoh's daughter finds the baby and has compassion. She takes care of him, and she even gets his own mom to nurse him! I guess considering all the things that could have happened, getting paid to nurse her own baby was a good thing for the mom—even though she had to give him up when he grew up. So the "bigger point" of this story may be how the Hebrews got stuck in a bad situation and how they got out of it. But what do you think?

Love,
Mom

34

Dear Mom,

Well, I don't think I would like to be tangled up in Moses' situation, but considering the story line, I think it all turned out for the best. Like, what if Moses had been killed? What would have happened to the Hebrews? And would there be a Bible, or would anyone even know there is a God? I also think Moses had an important role as a baby. He taught the Pharaoh's daughter to be considerate to all children, not just the royal ones.

Love,
Maggie

A DIFFERENT VIEW: MOSES *by Linda H. Hollies*

My first memories revolve around multiple loving mothers, lots of crying, and loads of loving care. I have never had only one mother or even one father. I know that sounds strange, but it's the honest truth. There were several mothers in my young life, as well as two distinctly different fathers. And I can vividly remember that many women in my birth community were always in grief because they could not be someone's mother.

The first "mother" I had besides my birth mother was my big sister, Miriam. She was just a girl when she watched over me in a little boat that my birth mother had made to hide me. There was a mean ruler who wanted all the boy babies of my race killed. I never understood why he wanted to kill all the newborn boys. What could a tiny baby do to harm a grown-up man with all kinds of power? But he had ruled that all Hebrew boy babies were to be killed while being born.

Miriam told me that two community midwives, Shiphrah and Puah, were called to the palace and told to murder all the male babies born to my people. These two women believed in the Almighty God, so, with quiet resistance, they became like second mothers to all the baby boys that they saved. They nurtured life in my community by refusing to carry out an order that would eventually have meant certain death for me.

Shiprah and Puah were really very smart and assertive women, who lived out their faith in God. They never said anything that sounded sassy or like backtalk to the ruler. They just agreed together that they would tell him they had arrived too late when women in our community were having children. After we left the land of slavery for our Promised Land, God rewarded them with land and families of their own.

When I think now of how courageous they were as women, I feel such pride and joy. Either one of these women could easily have gone along with the program. They could have caved in to the ruling idea that this mean man was really in charge of who should live and who should die. But our God is the one who created life, and these two women who helped to "mother" our community joined God in making sure life would continue for the Hebrews in Egypt. In order for me to grow up and lead our nation out of slavery, five different mothers had to care for me!

Of course my birth mother, Jochebed, (Ex. 6:20) was a really, really brave woman. Jochebed had already made up her mind that I was going to live. She used to tell me that God had spoken to her and told her I would be a special deliverer for our race. I didn't know what that meant, but I knew she loved me so much that she went to great lengths to save my life.

For three months, mother hid me in our home. When I grew to be too active for her to hide me any longer, she became an engineer. She knew I was supposed to be thrown into the river, but no one had said it couldn't be in a boat! She constructed a basket out of woven reeds caulked with pitch that became my "ark of safety." Mother put me into the little boat that she had made and told my sister-mother, Miriam, to stand guard on the shore to protect me. I know that Miriam got scared trying to make sure nothing happened to me. This prevented her from playing with her friends. She did not have the freedom to be a little girl. She had to "mother" me to keep me alive.

I cannot tell you what name I was given by my birth father, Amram. (Ex. 6:20) This has been a puzzle to me my whole life. Our Hebrew culture demanded that my father select my name, but the only name I know came from my adoptive mother, Pharaoh's daughter. She was an Egyptian, so when she pulled me out of my hiding place in the water, she gave me an Egyptian name, Moses. It means "saved from the water."

God has a great sense of humor, it seems to me. For it was my adoptive mother's father, the Pharaoh, who had made the rule that all boys like me were to be killed. Yet when my adoptive mother heard me crying, her heart went out to me. She said to her maid, "This must be one of the Hebrews' children." (Ex. 2:6) It was then that my smart big sister, Miriam, jumped out and asked her, "Do you want me to go and get a nursing mother from among the Hebrews for you?" The Pharaoh's daughter said yes to my sister, and do you know what? My sister went and got Jochebed to come and nurse me!

This is how I got to know the very best of both worlds. It was my family of origin that told me my history and taught me about our God. It was my birth mother who fed me with her milk, nurtured me, and told me repeatedly how very special I was to God's divine plan to deliver us from slavery. I did not have all the pieces of the giant puzzle, but my birth family had the chance to instill many Hebrew characteristics, traits, and values into my spirit.

My adoptive mother, whose name is never mentioned in the Scriptures, came to visit me often in the Hebrew slave ghetto. Sometimes she would have my biological mother bring me to the Pharaoh's palace for a visit. A little while ago, I came to live in the palace for good. Yes, the male child who was supposed to die came to live among the wealthy and the influential of Egypt. The hearts of kings must be in God's hand, for the Pharaoh accepted me! The very one who had made a rule to kill all male babies like me welcomed me into his inner chambers. This man became a father to me, a protector against harm, and a mentor, teaching me how to rule a nation.

All I have needed God has provided! My split living arrangement had to be part of God's divine plan too. Many days I will confess to being confused, for slaves like my birth parents don't know much about being in charge! Yet I'm learning all I need to know about politics, wealth, education, and management in the palace of the Pharaoh. I was ordained before my birth to lead God's chosen people into the Promised Land, so for a while I must live between two opposing worlds.

JEPHTHAH'S DAUGHTER

(Judges 11)

The daughter in this story is not given a name, but her amazing fate has created much controversy and her story has been interpreted in numerous ways by biblical scholars. Some say she was literally sacrificed as the victim of her father's rash vow. Others say she was a metaphorical sacrifice.[21] Still others say she is a female model of sacrificial love that points to Jesus' sacrifice. Her story has even been used to teach young women to mind their parents, no matter what! Significant grammatical ambiguities in the Hebrew story, as well as the inventiveness of interpreters today, make numerous readings possible.

As the story goes, a mighty warrior named Jephthah is driven away by his family. His brothers reject him because Jephthah's mother is a prostitute, not a legal wife like their mother, and they don't want to share their inheritance with him. Jephthah flees to the land of Tob and becomes the leader of a band of outlaws. (Judges 11:1-3) When the Israelites face attacks by the Ammonites, they need a strong commander to lead them out of the chaos and they approach Jephthah. Jephthah understandably taunts them: "Are you not the very ones who rejected me and drove me out of my father's house? So why do you come to me now when you are in trouble?" (Judges 11:7) Jephthah agrees to lead their struggle against the Ammonites, but only on the condition that he become their commander in chief.[22]

Jephthah's leadership begins immediately and is effective. He engages in a diplomatic showdown

Commentary
by Stephanie Biggs-Scribner

with the Ammonite king. (Judges 11:12)[23] He sends a message demonstrating the historical right of the Israelites to the land that the Ammonites are disputing with them. When his message is ignored, the spirit of God comes upon Jephthah and he marches off to war. Not content merely to trust in his own strength and the rightness of his cause, Jephthah makes a vow to God: "If you will give the Ammonites into my hand, then whoever comes out of the doors of my house to meet me, when I return victorious from the Ammonites, shall be the LORD'S, to be offered up by me as a burnt offering." (Judges 11:30b-31)

As it turns out, Jephthah is victorious, and the first one who comes out of his house to welcome him home is his only child, a daughter! (Judges 11:33-34) At this point Jephthah catches a glimpse of his error. He tears his clothes and says, "Alas, my daughter! You have brought me very low; you have become the cause of great trouble to me. For I have opened my mouth to the LORD, and I cannot take back my vow." (Judges 11:35) Notice that he blames the victim for a predicament he created himself.

Because of difficulties with the Hebrew in this story, speculation about the sacrifice of his daughter has been raised. Optional interpretations have arisen deeming her sacrifice to have been perpetual virginity. However, the story as we have it in Judges 11 says she was to become a burnt offering.

Before this nameless daughter is sacrificed, she requests two months to mourn with her companions the fact that she will die without ever having slept with a man or borne children. Jephthah concedes, and his daughter goes with her friends into the mountains. After her two months are up, she returns and Jephthah fulfills his vow. (Judges 11:39a)

The story concludes with the information that there is an annual four-day event during which the daughters of Israel gather to commemorate the sacrifice of Jephthah's daughter. (Judges 11:40) How long this custom survived in Israel is not known.

Today, rather than using this gruesome story of child sacrifice to scare children into good behavior,[24] readers find value in learning from the mistakes described in the story. If Jephthah had simply trusted God instead of trying to manipulate God into helping him, perhaps the victory would have been his without costing his daughter's life.

Joseph Jeter recommends that the story be used to call us into accountability for what we, socially speaking, have allowed to happen to our daughters.

He looks into the accounts of two different teenaged daughters in the Holocaust era and, citing this text along with numerous texts from the Gospels, Jeter asserts that "no offering that we can give to Jephthah's daughter...is acceptable...except resurrection!"[25]

No matter what type of sacrifice Jephthah's daughter was, she might represent women today who are sacrificed by discriminatory health-care systems, political policies, employment practices, and educational opportunities set up by and for men. If readers see the story in this way, who knows what types of social betterment may result? Jephthah's daughter may yet be resurrected!

LETTERS ON JEPHTHAH'S DAUGHTER
by Stephanie and Maggie Biggs-Scribner

Dear Maggie,

Of all the stories that are hard for me to tell you about, this one is the hardest. In the book of the Bible called Judges, there are lots of frightening stories. In fact, the book is so tough that lots of people—including me—think the book is "crisis literature." That is, it shows us how bad things can get when there is no good leader for the people.

In the story, there is a man named Jephthah whose mom was a prostitute. His dad is married and has sons. These sons do not like Jephthah because they don't think they should have to share their inheritance with the son of a prostitute. (Does that kind of greed sound familiar?) Jephthah goes to live somewhere else so that he won't have to deal with his half-brothers anymore. But pretty soon there is an attack against Israel from an outside group. The Israelites know that Jephthah would be a good commander to lead them through a war, so they send for him. Jephthah says something like, "Yeah, but aren't you the same people who sent me away, saying that I shouldn't inherit with you?"

Anyway, to make a long story short, Jephthah insists that if he helps them, he gets to be in charge of them. They agree. But when everything is going well, Jephthah is overcome by his own doubts. So he vows that, if

God will help him lead Israel to victory, whoever comes out of his house first to greet him when he comes home will be a burnt sacrifice to God! Well, he does lead his army to victory, and what do you know! It's his daughter who comes out to greet him! The story says that when Jephthah sees who it is, he rips his clothes in distress over having to sacrifice his only child. He says he feels terrible that she had to be the first one who came out to greet him. But—good grief!—think how terrible it was for her that she should have to be sacrificed just for dancing out to greet him!

This story has a lot of problems with it. Consider this: Jephthah pretty much knew it would be a female who came out to congratulate him. Other stories in the Bible show us that the women usually welcomed back the men when the men returned from war. A second point to consider is that he might have found a way to get out of his vow. Abraham did not have to sacrifice Isaac. A ram showed up just in time—perhaps because Abraham trusted God. Jephthah's daughter gets no ram.

She does have some friends, though, and she asks her dad for two months to spend with them in the mountains before the sacrifice. She gets the two months. Supposedly, the daughters of Israel remember her for four days every year by going away together in her honor.

But here's something that's a shame. Consider that moms—especially in our ancient tradition—felt like eternal life was really about being remembered after you died. If a mother felt that the only way she would have life after death was to be remembered by her kids, then what must the mom have felt like when her only daughter was sacrificed? In the story about Jephthah's daughter, the mother is never even mentioned! Talk about being forgotten! Well, she was forgotten, but her daughter wasn't.

So what do you think? Was Jephthah a bad parent for not figuring out what else he could do instead of sacrificing his daughter? Or did he show that he was a kind parent by tearing his clothes and by giving his daughter the two months she asked for? And what do you think about the mother?

Love, Mom

Dear Mom,

It was so unfair! The daughter died and the mother was forgotten. I think the people who wrote this story made a bad decision by not putting the mother in. If you are a mom or you can remember a lot about your childhood, you know the big role of a mom.

I think for Jephthah's daughter being sacrificed was both a horrible thing and a blessing. A horrible thing because there was maybe a one in a hundred chance she would be the first one to come out the door, yet it happened to be her. A blessing because she went to be with God, and she was blessed to be with God.

Love, Maggie

A DIFFERENT VIEW: JEPHTHAH'S DAUGHTER *by Linda H. Hollies*

Can you imagine going through life and through the pages of history without a name? I can distinctly tell you that it's no fun being remembered by the name of a father who used you as a sacrifice unto God. I can say without a doubt that it's no fun to be remembered not for what you did but for what was done to you!

My story begins with the words, "Now Jephthah the Gileadite, the son of a prostitute, was a mighty warrior." (Judges 11:1*a*) As you can imagine, I was born into a dysfunctional family. My father had issues. My mother had issues. And I was born into a climate where shame was at our very foundation. Shame does not set the stage for a good beginning in life. Shame is not a condition in which openness, trust, self-confidence, and self-esteem thrive. Shame produces folks who try to hide their issues behinds masks, pretenses, and grand schemes.

Since my father lived as an outsider in his father's family, his prime motivation was to be honored and accepted. I can remember him sitting alone, often holding his head in his hands, as my mother tried to bring him out of his slumps of despair. He seemed to spend much of his time drawing diagrams of war strategies. Winning was his only goal. Only winning would bring him honor and acceptance.

My father seldom spoke to us. We were only females. My mother never had any other children; and, like all men in Israel, my father wanted sons. Sure, he sometimes patted me on my head and smiled at me, but I cannot remember him ever doing any kind thing toward my mother. Surely you have noticed that my mother is not even mentioned in a sidebar! Sometimes my father would hold me and look at me as if trying to see if he could find value within me. But, as women, my mother and I were not his primary consideration.

Since my father was an outsider in his family, I often wondered how the marriage arrangers would find someone to offer the bride's price for me. Prostitutes had value among the male population as objects, but they didn't count as people when it came to rank and worth in the community. Everybody knew my family lineage, for my father had become a mighty warrior by the time I was born. Everyone knew what my grandmother was. In our tribe, there were few secrets.

I thought a lot about my future as a wife and a mother. Maybe another tribal chief would pay the bride's price for me. Perhaps there was a land where my grandmother's shame did not matter but the worth of my father's name and fame would make me a valuable acquisition. For the truth of the matter is that all wives were "acquired" to bring more wealth, more status, and more male heirs to their new family. There was hope for me that I could move so far away that the reputation of my grandmother would be diminished—maybe even erased. A girl could dream. When Dad was chosen as military leader of the whole tribe, I began to dream big dreams.

One day, I heard the sounds of chariots rumbling and I knew that my father was returning from another battle. My mother was busy trying to prepare a feast with the women in the cooking tents, so I ran outside to welcome the men home. It was the biggest mistake of my life! When my father saw me dancing up to him with my tambourine, he said, "Alas, my daughter! You have brought me very low; you have become the cause of great trouble to me. For I have opened my mouth to the LORD, and I cannot take back my vow." (Judges 11:35)

How was I to know that my father would make a vow unto God offering "whoever" first came out to greet him as a sacrifice of thanksgiving for a military victory? Now do you see how little a woman's worth was in Israel? Now do you understand the extremely low place of a female on the ladder of life? Do you begin to grasp how insignificant a girl child actually was if I could be included with "whatever" came out of our home?

I knew right then that there was a death warrant over my head! I realized that my future was over as of that moment! All my dreams, all my hopes, all my imaginings were dead. Because I came dancing out to welcome my father home, I became the living sacrifice for all of Israel. And my father placed all the blame on me!

This was the worst period of my short life. The shame of having a harlot for a grandmother didn't compare with the awfulness of the future that awaited me. My father had made a vow to God and could not take it back. So I began to think about what I needed to do to prepare for the ending of my earthly days. I began to grope for the meaning and purpose of life. I tried to consider what "the end" was going to mean for me. I told my father that I needed two months to go off into the mountains with my girlfriends to bring closure to my existence. I might have to be killed, but I wanted some "me time" before I died. My father arranged it and gave us permission to leave for two months.

Yes, I was the one who called the very first women's conference! I needed a group of women to surround me and wail with me. I needed a sisterhood who could understand my plight and share my grief over having to die before ever having had the chance to experience life in its fullness. So I called a gathering of girlfriends, and off to the high places we went.

This was a first in Israel, for virgins were guarded as prize possessions. All the other fathers must have known that no man would dare to try anything funny while we were unprotected. God was watching. So we were allowed to go into the mountains and to share our hopes and fears with one another. We talked about our dreams for the future. We talked about what we had wanted to happen to us as women. We sang together. We prayed together. And my friends grieved with me that I would never know the love of a husband or that of a child. They grieved with me that there would be no marriage, no new home to establish, and no childbirth to accomplish. Sometimes we forgot why we were there and felt free to laugh, to sleep, and to have fun. But sometimes, especially at night, death whispered among us. A chill would come over us, and the lamentations would begin all over again.

This gathering did not change my lot in life. It did not offer me the happiness that I so desired or give me an opportunity to forget about the death sentence upon my head. But it allowed a group of women to make some serious decisions about their limited range of options. It made us more aware of our gift of life and our potential for motherhood. And this gathering gave us an unprecedented chance to discuss, to hear, and to celebrate the collective wisdom of women.

My insistence upon this gathering established a yearly event. For four days each year, Israelite women would go off to spend quality time together and lament my passing. My short life and early death were not in vain!

ELIJAH AND THE WIDOW'S SON

(I Kings 17:1-24)

This story anticipates stories of miraculous healings in the New Testament. As in many other prophetic stories, compassion is shown for those who struggle to provide for themselves. A little background is needed. The story takes place during the reign of King Ahab over Israel. Ahab "did evil in the sight of the LORD more than all who were before him." (I Kings 16:30). He married the daughter of an idolatrous Sidonian, Jezebel, and he turned to worshiping her god, the idol Baal, for whom he erected a special altar and a sacred pole. (I Kings 16:31-33)

The prophet Elijah was sent to Ahab to announce that there would be no rain in the land for years until Elijah called for it. Of course, the drought impinged on Elijah too, so God told him to go and live by a wadi (oasis) in the wilderness. God sent ravens to feed him there. (I Kings 17:3-4)

Eventually even the wadi dried up, and Elijah received instructions from God to go up to Zarephath, where a widow would care for him.

Then the word of the LORD came to him, saying, "Go now to Zarephath, which belongs to Sidon, and live there; for I have commanded a widow there to feed you." So he set out and went to Zarephath. When he came to the gate of the town, a widow was there gathering sticks; he called to her and said, "Bring me a little water in a vessel, so that I may drink." As she was going to bring it, he called to her and said, "Bring me a morsel of bread in your hand." But she said,

Commentary
by Stephanie Biggs-Scribner

"As the LORD your God lives, I have nothing baked, only a handful of meal in a jar, and a little oil in a jug; I am now gathering a couple of sticks, so that I may go home and prepare it for myself and my son, that we may eat it, and die." (I Kings 17:8-12)

Her statement that she and her son will eat and then die is an oddity that catches the attention of readers. Perhaps she was intending to celebrate one last meal and then take her own life and the life of her son to escape slow starvation. It is not likely that her remark is merely a response to Elijah's request for help. She has very little food, and she makes it clear that she plans to prepare what little she has for herself and her son only.

Elijah's initial demand for water and food seems pushy. He does not greet her, does not explain who he is, and does not politely request the water of her. Rather, he tells her to get him some water. And now that she has made it clear that she has only a handful of food and intends to use it for her son and herself, abrasive Elijah does not seem to get the message. He not only reiterates his request but also tells her to provide food for him first! He says, "Do not be afraid; go and do as you have said; but first make me a little cake of it and bring it to me, and afterwards make something for yourself and your son." (I Kings 17:13)

In light of his crude speaking manner, his instructing her not to be afraid would seem offensive if it were not followed up by a prophetic guarantee. Elijah says to her, "Thus says the LORD, the God of Israel: The jar of meal will not be emptied and the jug of oil will not fail until the day that the LORD sends rain on the earth." (I Kings 17:14)

Elijah's guarantee seems strange. He gives her no date by which to expect that rain will come, and the promise from a prophet—that her food will last until rain comes—creates a curious situation. If she complies with his wishes and provides for two adults plus a child in order to see Elijah's promise fulfilled, she will wind up hoping that rain never comes—a hope that is the opposite of the hope she had before she met Elijah.

Whatever her thoughts are, the widow agrees to provide for him. Her food supply, which was recently minuscule, is miraculously made into enough to care for the three[26] of them for days. (I Kings 17:15) But disaster follows closely behind this miracle of divine providence; for, after this miracle, the woman's son becomes ill. His illness grows worse until there is "no breath left in him." (I Kings 17:17b) Having seen Elijah's ability to communicate with God, the woman now blames Elijah for the death of her son. "What have you against me, O man of God?" she asks. "You have come to me to bring my sin to remembrance, and to cause the death of my son!" (I Kings 17:18) Her pain-filled remark that her son has died because of her sin indicates that she thinks perhaps her son's death comes from Elijah's God.

The prophet is moved by her pain. In a miracle that resembles many in the New Testament, he resuscitates the boy (I Kings 17:19-22). But before the prophet performs this miracle, he expresses his own shock and confusion at the situation. He cries out, "O LORD my God, have you brought calamity even upon the widow with whom I am staying, by killing her son?" (I Kings 17:20)

After performing a series of unusual actions, Elijah successfully brings the boy back to life.

He took him from her bosom, carried him up into the upper chamber where he was lodging, and laid him on his own bed.... Then he stretched himself upon the child three times, and cried out to the LORD, "O LORD my God, let this child's life come into him again." The LORD listened to the voice of Elijah; the life of the child came into him again, and he revived. (I Kings 17:19, 21-22)

The precise description of Elijah's actions seems peculiar. He stretches himself out upon the boy, not next to him. He does this three times, as if repetition brings the desired results. Moreover, though he could have used other terms, he uses the divine name to call upon God. Did hearers of this story presume God's name itself to be powerful? This seems to be the case. And certainly the mother's words when she sees her son restored to life attribute power to the speech of Elijah: "Now I know that you are a man of God, and that the word of the LORD in your mouth is truth." (I Kings 17:24)

In this story of Elijah's bringing a deceased child back to life, there is much to be considered about the way divine power is characterized. Elijah and the widow both make accusations against God, and yet God responds with compassion and brings the boy back to life. The story is a precursor of other stories of resurrection to be recounted in the Christian Scriptures, such as the raising of Lazarus (John 11:1-45), the resuscitation of Jairus's daughter (Matt. 9:18-26, Mark 5:22-43, Luke 8:41-56), and, of course, the resurrection of Jesus on the third day, which is reminiscent of the three times Elijah calls on God to raise the widow's son.

LETTERS ON ELIJAH AND THE WIDOW'S SON

by Stephanie and Maggie Biggs-Scribner

Dear Maggie,

This story is about a widow woman with only one child—a son. A prophet named Elijah comes to the woman to get food and water while he is doing some work for God. The woman does not have very much food left, and she wants to make sure that she and her son get to eat it. Elijah insists that she feed him—Elijah—first! But he promises that, if she does as he says, she will not run out of food until the rains come again. She does feed him first and continues to make meals for him. Everything seems to be working out fine.

But then something terrible happens—her son dies! She gets mad at God and at Elijah, since Elijah is God's prophet. Elijah did not make the boy die, and he is confused about why the boy died, too. So he takes the boy and revives him, and he does it in a weird way. He lies on top of him three times and prays: "O LORD my God, let this child's life come into him again." God listens and the boy comes back to life.

The woman is surprised and says that now she knows for certain that Elijah is a man of God. I'm sure I would be surprised too! We never get to know the names of the mom and the boy. They are just ordinary people like you and me. So God works miracles for ordinary people too—not just for people who are going to be kings! How about that?

Love, Mom

Dear Mom,
I definitely know I would be surprised. In fact, I'd be freaked out if my son had died and then all of a sudden he's alive again. Uhhhh....I'm getting the creeps just thinking about it.

Love, Maggie

A DIFFERENT VIEW OF ELIJAH AND THE WIDOW'S SON: THE SON OF A SINGLE WORKING MOTHER by Linda H. Hollies

My mom says that I'm her doubly blessed child. I know that every mother feels her child is a blessing, especially after her husband dies. But Mom's not just talking about the fact that I keep her company and remind her of my father. Mom says I was born to her at the right time and place.

I don't know how many single mothers would say this, knowing how hard it is to take care of themselves without men around to protect them. My mom really does work hard. She is not a woman of Israel. As a matter of fact, both she and I were born in the same area as that blood-thirsty Queen Jezebel, who is killing off all the Hebrew God's prophets. We worshiped the idol Baal, so my mom had no promises from the Most High God to comfort her in hard times. And when I was a baby, our land was in dire straits.

The Hebrew prophet Elijah had gotten a message from his God to tell King Ahab and Queen Jezebel that there would be no rain in the land for years. This brought about a severe famine, and even the water in the lakes began to dry up. My mom had enough food stored up for us to eat for some time. We didn't eat three times a day, but Mom could still make hot bread and we had water to drink at least once a day.

I was often hungry, but I wasn't going to complain. My mom would be out for many hours looking for more food. She was always tired, but she played games with me to try and take my attention off the grumbling in my empty stomach. I heard Mom's stomach rumbling too, but she would make sure I had eaten enough before she would even touch her little cake of bread.

One day Mom told me that she was going to gather the kindling wood to cook our last meal. When she said "last meal," she had a really sad look in her eyes. Mom's eyes had been sad for as long as I could remember. I often thought that missing my father and having to work so hard to take care of me by herself made her sad, but this time there was something extra sad about Mom as she left to get the wood. The trees were dry from lack of rain, so my mom wasn't gone long looking for dead branches. When she came in, I could hear her talking to herself.

"Who does he think he is asking me to fix him a cake before I feed my own son or feed myself? I told that vagrant all we had was enough to cook and to eat our last meal. Doesn't that fool know there's a famine in the land? Doesn't he understand that I'm a poor widow with a child to feed? And doesn't he understand that we're not kinfolks and we don't serve the same God? He must be crazy! Or else he thinks I'm crazy!" I know this is what Mom said, for she kept repeating it.

I had never seen that look on her face before. She was scurrying around, trying to get the meal and the oil together for a little cake. It was starting to smell good, and I was really hungry. I sat and watched my mom cook that first cake. It was larger than the ones we had been eating, and I didn't see much meal or oil left over. I hoped that Mom was fixing that big cake for me. But when she finished, she carried it out the door!

She wasn't gone too long. That "vagrant," as she called him, must have been close to our place. She came back with another strange look on her face as she reached way down to get more meal out of the bottom of the barrel. I wish I could explain the look of shock on my mom's face as she came up with a big handful. The oil jar, too, had been almost empty, but the oil kept flowing. Mom made me two big cakes, and she ate two big cakes. Then my mom took my hands, pulled me up on my feet, and began to dance me around the room in a crazy jig. All my mom kept saying was: "That man is a prophet. That man is a prophet. That man is a prophet."

When Mom had fixed the prophet another cake and taken it out to him, she asked him if he wanted to come into our home. He moved upstairs into what had been the room planned for me. His name was Elijah. He told my mother that he was running for his life, trying to hide from Queen Jezebel. I thought it was a joke. Why would a person try to hide in the very place Queen Jezebel came from? It didn't make any sense to me, and yet he lived with us for over three years without being caught.

Every day that the prophet was with us, we all ate three full meals. And if visitors came to our home, Mom would feed them too. The meal barrel and the oil jar always looked nearly empty, but every time my mom reached in to bring something up, it was there. In a time of famine, in a land where folks were starving to death, the man of God saved our lives and taught us about the power of the Almighty God. He taught us how to pray. He taught us how to believe in miracles. That's what he called our food, a miracle.

The prophet even told us that God had been feeding him down by a lake until he was sent to find my mother and me. Can you believe that his God would send him to the very homeland of Queen Jezebel and direct him to find my mother? My mom said it was because of me that God had sent the prophet. She called me her blessing, for the prophet told my mother that his God had compassion upon little children and women who did favors like my mom had done for him.

My mother taught me always to be respectful and obedient to adults. I think that's why she was so quick to follow the prophet's request down by the village gates. My mom was always nice and respectful. She had lots of love in her heart. And she didn't have to work so hard when the prophet stayed with us. We had lots of time to sit and talk and listen to the man of God—that's what we began to call him.

One day I had a fever. My mother told me to stay on my pallet in her room. I blacked out for a while, and when I came to, the man of God was lying on top of me on the big bed in his room, talking to his God. My mother was jumping up and down, yelling and screaming: "Thank you, God! Thank you, God! Thank you, God!" She had tears on her face and the biggest smile I'd ever seen.

When the man of God lifted me off his bed and handed me to my mother, she squeezed me so tightly I could hardly breathe. She kept kissing me over and over. Every now and then, she'd say it again: "Thank you, God!" The man of God just shook his head and went back into his room until it was time for our next meal.

My mom really became a believer in miracles after the man of God brought me back to life by breathing his breath into my nose and mouth. He told us that this was how the Creator had put life into Adam and Eve. He told us the creation story at dinner that night. I often asked him to tell it to me again before he left our house when the famine was over. I liked that story. I liked the man of God. I liked his God. We never again went to worship Baal.

THE DEAL-MAKING MOTHERS

(II Kings 6:24-33)

This story of children and their mothers is meant to convey tragic national circumstances, as well as the inadequacy of the nation's political leader, an unnamed king of Israel. Because of the king's helplessness, two women wind up cannibalizing one of their sons! This story about cannibalism of children committed by their mothers is probably not intended to convey any one particular historical event. Numerous other biblical accounts that feature the same theme of cannibalism[27] attest to the reality that starving people sometimes resorted to eating each other in ancient Israel.[28]

The background of the story is that Israel's capital, the walled city of Samaria, is suffering a great famine because it has been besieged for a long time by the Syrians under King Ben-hadad. (II Kings 6:24)

As the siege continued, famine in Samaria became so great that a donkey's head was sold for eighty shekels of silver, and one-fourth of a kab of dove's dung for five shekels of silver. Now as the king of Israel was walking on the city wall, a woman cried out to him, "Help, my lord king!" He said, "No! Let the LORD help you. How can I help you? From the threshing floor or from the wine press?" But then the king asked her, "What is your complaint?" She answered, "This woman said to me, 'Give up your son; we will eat him today, and we will eat my son tomorrow.' So we cooked my son and ate him. The next day I said to her, 'Give up your son and we will eat him.' But she has hidden

Commentary
by Stephanie Biggs-Scribner

her son." When the king heard the words of the woman he tore his clothes—now since he was walking on the city wall, the people could see that he had sackcloth on his body underneath—and he said, "So may God do to me, and more, if the head of Elisha son of Shaphat stays on his shoulders today." So he dispatched a man from his presence.

Now Elisha was sitting in his house, and the elders were sitting with him. Before the messenger arrived, Elisha said to the elders, "Are you aware that this murderer has sent someone to take off my head? When the messenger comes, see that you shut the door and hold it closed against him. Is not the sound of his master's feet behind him?" While he was still speaking with them, the king came down to him and said, "This trouble is from the LORD! Why should I hope in the LORD any longer?" (II Kings 6:25-33).

Verse 25, which speaks of the price of a donkey's head and a few pints of dove's dung, illustrates the severity of the famine. This information shows how people were so hungry that even a "repulsive item" of food like a donkey's head or dove's dung had become extraordinarily valuable.[29]

An unnamed king[30] passing on the ramparts is appealed to for help by a woman, who is also unnamed. (II Kings 6:26) Before even hearing her request, the king blows her off with a brusque refusal—"No! Let the LORD help you. How can I help you?"—and a question about whether she expects him to help her from the threshing floor (give her grain) or from the wine press. (II Kings 6:27) This sarcastic question is meant to express his inability to do anything for her. Surprisingly, however, he immediately changes his attitude and asks, "What is your complaint?"[31] (II Kings 6:28)

She explains that she and another woman made a deal to eat her son on one day and then the son of the other woman on the next day. Her son was boiled and eaten, but when she asked for her share of the other woman's son the next day, the second woman hid her son instead.

The king is overwhelmed by the news and tears his clothes, whereupon the people below see that he has been wearing sackcloth beneath his royal robes.[32] The king swears to behead Elisha for having warned him of God's punishment—as though beheading the messenger will fix the problem. He sends a man to do the job for him, and he follows shortly after to see the outcome.

Elisha somehow knows that the king is on his way. He says to the elders with him, "Are you aware that this murderer has sent someone to take off my head? When the messenger comes, see that you shut the door and hold it closed against him." (II Kings 6:32b) The chapter ends when the king suddenly appears. Rather than beheading Elisha, the king blurts out, "This trouble is from the LORD! Why should I hope in the LORD any longer?" (II Kings 6:33) This question spurs the reader to continue into chapter 7. However, as our concern is with the children, we will return to the situation of the woman who entreats the king. Though it is not the most disturbing topic to address, we will begin by asking where the fathers are. In Deuteronomy 28:49-57, parents' being so hungry that they cannibalize their own children is predicted as punishment for not obeying the LORD. The gruesome scenario is described in great detail in the Deuteronomy passage.

In Deuteronomy 28:53, daughters, too, are listed as those who will be cannibalized. In light of the emphasis the Bible places on a woman's desire to bear sons, the fact that only sons and not daughters are mentioned in II Kings 6 shows the most extreme possible reversal of motherly instinct. It is yet another way this story illustrates the desperate situation inside the city walls.

Ezekiel 5:10 says, "Surely parents shall eat their children in your midst, and children shall eat their parents" as a punishment for not having followed God's statutes. Men are included in both of these dire predictions, but the story in II Kings 6 mentions only women. They are not described as prostitutes as are the women in I Kings 3:16-27, where Solomon judges between two complainants as to which is the real mother of a disputed child. Neither are they called widows, as we might have expected after the siege of their city. So where are the fathers? Is the narrator saying that this text exemplifies what, for him, are women's problems? Who is responsible? Who is blamed? Who mourns, and for what loss?

In a terrible famine, it cannot be expected that the two sons would have lived long. Lamentations 2:11-12 describes the wretched situation of the remnant in Jerusalem during the captivity. Seeing the suffering of the children and infants makes the writer of Lamentations feel physically ill. If the mothers in our own story felt the same distress over watching their infants suffer, the idea of mercy killing cannot be ruled out.

There is no way around it—this story is disturbing. Gender politics aside, the point of the story is that children, the most vulnerable members of society, suffer the most when a nation is disobedient to God. The message of this story for current world leaders ought to be sobering.

LETTERS ON THE DEAL-MAKING MOTHERS
by Stephanie and Maggie Biggs-Scribner

Dear Maggie,

The last story I told you about was a happy one, where God and a prophet bring a boy back to life. This story has a prophet in it, too, but it is not going to be a happy story. This time the prophet is Elisha, the successor of Elijah. The king of Israel has been disobedient to God, so his city is being besieged by the King of Syria. This means that the Syrian army has the city surrounded and won't let anybody in or out. Eventually the people inside the city walls run out of food.

There are two mothers in the city who have little sons. One mother says to the other, "We'll eat your son today and tomorrow we'll eat mine." Can you believe that? Well, they eat the one woman's son, but the second day the mom who thought up the idea hides her son. So the mom whose son was eaten goes to the king for help. He rips his clothing in distress. I guess he's shocked, too! The king blames God for the terrible things that have happened to the people, so he gets mad at God's prophet, Elisha, and plans to kill him. Elisha avoids being killed by telling the king that the siege will be lifted the next day and that there will be plenty to eat again.

Personally, I think the story is meant to show us that when a society does not have good values, the kids suffer the most. And it works the other way too. How well a society treats its kids predicts the success of the whole society. What happens to the kids is like a heartbeat—you know when doctors have a person hooked up to a heart monitor and the monitor shows the heartbeat? I think that kids in the Bible stories—especially the ones in this story—are like the heartbeat on a monitor: they are the signs of a society's life. In this case, the society's life isn't going very well, so the beat wavers and weakens.

What do you think?

Love,
Mom

Dear Mom,

I personally don't know what I think. Ok, I do. Ummm...I feel sad and grossed out. That about wraps it up. I do wonder why one mom would promise to let her son be eaten and then break her promise and just stop the flow. I can see why you wouldn't want your son to get killed and eaten, but then don't kill somebody else's son and eat them.

Love, Maggie

A DIFFERENT VOICE: THE HIDDEN BABY *by Linda H. Hollies*

Sssh! Come really close. My mother has hidden me so that I will not be served as the evening meal. Yes, you heard me right. I'm not kidding and I'm not trying to play a joke on you. Yesterday, my mother and another woman ate that woman's child, and today it's supposed to be my turn. But my mother has had a change of heart, so she's hidden me away from the other hungry mother.

I was born to a woman starving in the city of Samaria. Our nation, Israel, has been separated from Judah for years and our people have decided to follow the gods of other nations. As a punishment, God has let the Syrian army surround our city. No one can go outside the city walls to get food. People are dying of starvation. The head of a donkey and the dung of a bird are sold in the market for a high price. It's one of the worst situations that our land has ever seen.

Many days I was hungry in my mother's womb. I can't tell you where my father is, for many of the men have disappeared. My mother made every attempt to find food just so she could bring me into the world. She has stolen food, and she has also eaten unspeakable things. There were many days when she could not find anything to eat at all. When she was hungry, so was I. It's hard to produce a robust, strong baby when you don't have enough to eat. Yet the maternal instincts of my mother and her pregnant friend kept them trying to stay alive for the sake of their babies.

Mom and her friend were desperate women. Nothing was going right. The nation was at war, the political system was all messed up, and even the leaders of the land were not in touch with God. When the economy breaks down, people turn on each other. When the legal system does not work, human beings become like wild animals. When no religious leader steps up to help people make good decisions, people begin to live according to their own devices in order to survive. When I was born, the world was in chaos.

God was not happy with the people of Israel. The prophet of God had tried to warn them that disaster was on the way, yet the people continued trying to make it on their own. Our king was in a losing battle with God, and all of us were suffering the dire consequences! When God is absent, nothing good will happen.

It's a difficult struggle to be born. It requires all the energy we babies can muster, and the only way we survive after birth is through our mother's milk. Mothers must be well-nourished to make good milk. Since the government systems were not working, there was no way for my mother or the other women to fill their empty cupboards. The religious systems were not offering plans whereby a community could pull together. The name of God was not being lifted in earnest supplication. Everyone was trying to make it without help.

When things begin to go wrong in a nation, women and their children are always the first ones who suffer. Women are needed to become mommies, for without children there will be no one to work the fields, gather the crops, or grow up to lead the people. But for some reason women and their children are not viewed as important, only as necessary. It's not fair. And it isn't just.

Mothers have special needs: nutritious food, help with their household chores, and encouragement when the time comes for them to give birth. They also need people to help them learn how to care for a newborn. No one was around to teach my mother how to be a good mommy. Plus, she was weak from having had to push me into the world all alone. In addition to that, she was slowly starving to death!

When you have a full stomach, your mind can work at full capacity. When you have been fed, all of your bodily systems work together, helping you make the best decisions for the time. But when your basic needs for food and shelter are not met, nothing else is important. When your stomach has hunger pangs and you don't have any idea where your next meal will come from, you can't think straight.

My mom and her friend did not seek a godly solution. They did not pray to the God of Israel for intervention. Instead, my mom and her friend made a horrible decision in an effort to save themselves. Yesterday, my mom and her friend boiled her friend's son and ate him! I couldn't believe it! They ate their own flesh and blood! Heathen nations had done this before, but our nation hadn't had to do this when it was obedient to God. Now God was angry about our nation's disobedience, so the grossest thing that has ever been heard of happened in our home.

Early this morning, my mother felt the return of her maternal instincts. During the wee hours, as the other mother slept with a full stomach, satisfied that I would be her next meal, my mother stole me away and hid me in order to save my life. Now there is a horrible fight going on between my mom and her friend. As a matter of fact, the other woman went to ask the king of Israel to back her up. All he did was tear his clothes. He hates the idea of parents eating their children, but even he has no influence with his God. The world has turned completely upside down. Where is my help?

Sssh...God is being quiet. Sssh...my mommy is being quiet. Sssh...I'm being really quiet too!

JAIRUS'S DAUGHTER

(Matthew 9:18-26; Mark 5:22-43)

The stories of Jairus's daughter found in Matthew 9 and Mark 5 are very similar, yet they are not exact duplicates. In Mark's version, Jairus, a leader of the synagogue, approaches Jesus to say that his daughter is very ill. Jesus starts to go with Jairus to see to the needs of the sick child, but he is interrupted by a woman with a hemorrhage. (Mark 5:25-34) Once the hemorrhage has been healed and Jesus has told the woman that her faith has made her well, some people come to announce to Jairus that his daughter is already dead. (Mark 5:35) At this point, the story shifts from the topic of a parent worried about a dying child to the topic of his fear, *phobou*, which can be counteracted by faith, *pisteue*. (Mark 5:36)

As in Mark's story, a woman with a hemorrhage interrupts Matthew's story of a leader of the synagogue whose daughter has just died. The fact that this interruption occurs in both stories would indicate that the daughter in Matthew 9 is the same as the one in Mark 5, although Matthew does not name the girl's father. In Matthew, the woman's hemorrhage is healed by faith, and then the story of the seemingly dead daughter healed through her father's faith is followed by a story of two blind men healed through their faith in Jesus' power, thus continuing the writer's focus on the topic of faith.

In both the Matthew and the Mark stories, Jesus goes to the synagogue leader's house, chases away the mourners (in Matthew, some of them are playing the flute), and declares that the child is not dead, only sleeping.

Commentary
by Stephanie Biggs-Scribner

And they laughed at him. Then he put them all outside, and took the child's father and mother and those who were with him [Peter, James, and John] and went in where the child was. He took her by the hand and said to her, "Talitha, cum," which means, "Little girl, get up!" And immediately the girl got up and began to walk about (she was twelve years of age). At this they were overcome with amazement. He strictly ordered them that no one should know this, and told them to give her something to eat. (Mark 5:40-43)

Jesus frequently charged the recipients of his miracles not to tell anyone, perhaps because he knew that the quickest way to have the whole region hear about what he had done was to forbid people to tell the secret.

Scholars have offered numerous explanations for the different details in Mark's and Matthew's versions of the story, and their scholarship is important to the study of Christ's life. But this book does not focus on the development of biblical stories. Rather, we are attempting to gain insight into the ways children have been portrayed in the Bible. The important point about both Mark's and Matthew's stories of this daughter is that her restoration to life comes within a mass of other stories about miracles. Not only do these examples reinforce the assumption that the health of children has long been important to parents, but they also show that the Christian community has understood God as having similar concerns about the health of children.

Another important point about the story of this daughter concerns the oddity of the story's interruption by the woman with the hemorrhage. Musa Dube reads the story of Jairus's daughter and the story of the woman with the hemorrhage as complementary pieces of the same unit. In her interweaving of the stories, Dube finds parallels with the experience of Africans under colonialism. Dube's main character, "Mama Africa," spends years traveling from one doctor to another seeking healing for her excessive bleeding. This bleeding symbolizes the drainoff of Africa's resources into foreign lands under colonialism. But Mama Africa needs more than just her own healing; she also seeks healing for her children. Overcome with anger and craving hope, Mama Africa cries out to her dying children, "Talitha cum," which means "Little girl, arise!"[33] She has watched her children suffer and die over and over again. Impoverished by doctor visits yet still weak and bleeding, she learns that Jesus Christ, "the healer of all diseases," is passing by.

She heard that Jesus was on his way to heal a little child already dead, the daughter of Jairus. Mama Africa is standing up. She is not talking. She is not asking. She is not offering any more money—for none is left. Mama Africa is coming behind Jesus. She is pushing through a strong human barricade. *Weak and still bleeding but determined, she is stretching out her hand. If only she can touch the garments of Jesus Christ!* [34] *(Italics are Musa Dube's.)*

Dube's use of this story responds well to current African needs and helps explain why Jairus's daughter is never named in the Scripture. The daughter in this story could be anyone's daughter. She could be the friend of anyone's daughter. She could be a nation. She could even be an entire continent.

LETTERS ABOUT JAIRUS'S DAUGHTER
by Stephanie and Maggie Biggs-Scribner

Dear Maggie,

I'm excited to tell you the next story—I think you'll like it! It's a story about the daughter of a man named Jairus. His daughter is sick, and Jairus is afraid that she's not going to get well. He goes to Jesus and asks him to come and heal her. Jesus starts to go with him to where the daughter is, but on the way, a lady interrupts them by touching the hem of Jesus' robe. Jesus feels some power go through him to heal her, and he stops and asks who touched him.

Preachers like to give sermons on the lady who touched Jesus' robe (they usually call it a "garment"), because it was her act of faith that led to her healing. But in the bigger story, the lady acts as a sort of interruption. She holds back Jesus and Jairus on their way to heal the daughter. Now, the story doesn't say what Jairus thought when she interrupted. I personally would have been annoyed at first, because if you were the sick one, I wouldn't have wanted to stop! But when I saw that a lady had been healed of excessive bleeding she had suffered from for twelve years just by touching Jesus, I would have been excited! If Jesus could do that without even trying, just think what he could do for you!

Of course before Jairus had time to get excited, some people came up to him and said not to bother Jesus anymore because his daughter was dead! When Jesus heard that, he told Jairus not to be afraid but just to believe. You can imagine Jairus's emotional swings between despair and hope as Jesus went with him to where his daughter was. When they got there, everybody was crying and making a commotion because the girl was dead. Jesus chased them away, saying she wasn't dead, just asleep. They actually laughed at him! But when Jesus walked into her room and said, "Talitha, cum" ("Little girl, get up!"), she came back to life and got up. Her parents were really surprised!

This story gives me hope that God works miracles and that people who care can sometimes be used by God to bring about miracles. You know that right now there isn't any cure for diseases like the one I have (multiple sclerosis), and I haven't really been expecting a miracle. But I do believe that miracles happen. And I do believe that with everybody working together, we can make things better. Seeing people try hard and work together to find a cure gives me hope. Plus I know that little miracles of healing are happening all the time in all of our bodies—yours, mine, and everybody else's. God designed our bodies to heal themselves of most things. Maggie, I know I've given you a lot to think about with all of this, so just pick what is on your mind the most and write to me about it. Okay?

Love,
Mom

Dear Mom,
I think the lady who touched Jesus might have had tons of faith, and that's why that miracle happened. Or else she had basically no faith, and to convince her to have faith, Jesus made a big miracle happen so that everyone who saw it would believe.

Love,
Maggie

A DIFFERENT VIEW: JAIRUS'S DAUGHTER *by Linda H. Hollies*

The silence was so sweet. There was a calm stillness in the atmosphere. I experienced a lightness and a brilliance that cannot be described. I can't honestly say that there was anyone around me in the brilliance, but I was not afraid. I didn't hear anyone in the stillness, but the quiet was not scary at all.

For almost a week I had been growing weaker and weaker. I couldn't eat my favorite dishes, which my mother kept having the cook prepare for me. I couldn't even sip the cool water that the servant would bring me in a gourd. The last thing I remembered was that my father had promised he was going to find the Teacher, a man who might be able to make me well. But I kept slipping deeper and deeper into the sweet silence.

My whole life had been full of excitement. I was the only child of a father and a mother who loved me but had many responsibilities. The children of our servants and of my relatives were everywhere, so I was always running, tumbling, tossing, skipping, and jumping as part of a crowd. My father spent many hours at the synagogue, and my mother was busy with overseeing our busy household. I tried to stay out of her sight, for she was determined that I was going to become a "young lady" and I wanted no part of that routine.

After having watched some of my older girl-friends learn to bow before men and to talk softly and to run a kitchen and to set a table for a meal, I knew that this was not my idea of fun. The fact that young women were supposed to spend hours being taught to walk correctly and to smile and to give the impression of being dainty was for somebody else, not me. I enjoyed my freedom and wanted no part of that growing up stuff. Being 12, I knew I had little time left to roam freely with the boys and girls, but I was not ready to abandon the adventurous life. I enjoyed every day to the fullest.

Yes, I even enjoyed the scribe who came to teach us every weekday. Being part of a ruling family, I was required to learn the reading, writing, and basic math needed to manage a household for a husband and family. I found the classes to be fun, and by the time the sun was high, we were dismissed for play. So far, this was the best year of my life. Little did I know that things would soon take a turn for the worse.

When I awoke one morning, I felt dizzy and sick to my stomach. It seemed as if I might have eaten something that was spoiled. My maid tried several home remedies, but they did not stop my dizziness and vomiting. Finally, my mother had to be called. She sent a servant to bring back the local physician, who gave me a tonic that he guaranteed would have me on my feet by the next morning. When it didn't work, he said, "Maybe God has a plan that is bigger than my tonic." The next morning, I was worse. I was still dizzy and had a case of dry heaves. It was not a good day for me.

My mother never left my bedside. I tried to tell her that I was feeling better, but her cool hand against my burning forehead told her a different story. She wet a towel and constantly bathed my face, but I began to feel the coming of the silence. Perhaps because of my inability to eat, or maybe because of the fever, my mother sent for the physician again, and this time she also sent for my father. I knew then that something serious had to be wrong with me, for she never disturbed my father at his business. The stillness was growing louder and louder as my mother and those others in my room seemed to be moving farther and farther away.

Scenes from recent days entered the stillness. I could see and talk to my friends. Even my animals ran across my mind. I could dimly hear my mother weeping and feel the servants scurrying. My father bent down to kiss my forehead and whispered, "Little One, I'm going to find a man who can make you well. I promise." I tried to answer him, but it seemed as if the stillness had taken control of my being. It might sound silly, but I can only say that the stillness was growing and I seemed to be getting smaller and smaller.

How I wanted to comfort my mother and my former nurse! I wanted to tell them I was feeling better. I wanted them to stop crying, but I could not reach them through the sweet stillness that had me in its hold. It never crossed my mind that I was dying. Age 12 was too young for me to think about death. Age 12 was when I was supposed to begin womanhood lessons. I was not old enough even to be thinking about boys—let alone to become a wife and mother. Surely 12 was too young for dying! Yet the stillness would not release me. It held me in a viselike grip.

I struggled to move, but I couldn't. I attempted to talk, but I couldn't. I lay there, and I could see and hear all the people who were in the room, but I could not for the life of me respond to tell them I was really all right. There was this feeling of being there and not being there at all. I wanted to laugh, but it wasn't funny. I wanted to cry, but I couldn't concentrate on what there was to cry about. So I lay there and listened to the sweetness of the silence that began to grow deeper and deeper within me.

Dying is not about struggling to live. Dying is accepting the silence and becoming one with it—or maybe becoming at one in it. The stillness finally became solid, and I could not hear or see anyone anymore. The last sounds I heard outside of the stillness were the loud, piercing screams of my mother and our family and friends. Not even the fact that my father was a leader of the synagogue had been able to save me.

"Talitha, cum!" ("Little girl, get up!"): these words drifted through to me from beyond the bounds of the stillness. "Talitha, cum!"—louder this time. The command went beyond, around, and through the layers holding me and pulled me toward wakefulness. "Talitha, cum!" The power within the words brought life into my stillness, and the powerful majesty of the voice demanded my immediate response. When I opened my eyes, there stood my parents with the Teacher called Jesus. There was a great commotion outside my room, as the professional wailers had already arrived. The news of my death had begun to circulate throughout the area.

The Teacher never asked me how I felt. The Teacher did not touch my head to see if the fever was gone. The Teacher simply stood there gazing at me, reaching out his hand. When he took my hand to pull me up, the sound of the stillness vanished completely. The Teacher was smiling at me with a gentle look of loving care. He instructed my bewildered folks to give me something to eat. And was I ever hungry!

As mother dispatched a servant to bring me a meal, my father stood weeping, holding onto both the Teacher and me. My mother still had a stunned look on her face when she returned to touch my forehead and to stroke my hand. The Teacher explained that the Ancient of Days was a life-giver, a way-maker, and a healer. He said that I had been brought to life for a purpose but to tell no one for now. None of us knew exactly what he was talking about, but we knew that he was special, and we all wanted to know more about the power he had displayed. This was the beginning of our walk of faith as committed believers in Christ. All of our lives were transformed by my resurrection from the dead!

Many people had doubts when the disciples of the Teacher began to spread the word that he had arisen after his crucifixion. You can bet my family never had any doubt! I am living proof of new life, new days, and new hope after death!

CHILDREN WHO SHOW ENTERPRISE

THE CAPTIVE GIRL

(II Kings 5)

The following passage tells the story of a Syrian man healed of leprosy through the enterprise of an Israelite slave girl working for his wife.

Naaman, commander of the army of the king of Aram, was a great man and in high favor with his master, because by him the LORD had given victory to Aram. The man, though a mighty warrior, suffered from leprosy. Now the Arameans on one of their raids had taken a young girl captive from the land of Israel, and she served Naaman's wife. She said to her mistress, "If only my lord were with the prophet who is in Samaria! He would cure him of his leprosy." So Naaman went in and told his lord just what the girl from the land of Israel had said. And the king of Aram said, "Go then, and I will send along a letter to the king of Israel." (II Kings 5:1-5a)

When the king of Israel reads the letter and learns that Naaman has come to him for healing, he rips his clothes and says, "Am I God, to give death or life, that this man sends word to me to cure a man of his leprosy? Just look and see how he is trying to pick a quarrel with me." (II Kings 5:7) Elisha hears that the king has torn his clothes in helplessness. He sends a message that the king should let Naaman come to him so that Naaman "may learn that there is a prophet in Israel." (II Kings 5:8)

The rest of the story concerns Naaman's refusal to believe that simply washing in the waters of the Jordan River, as Elisha has instructed him, is potent enough to make him well. Naaman says, "Are not Abana and Pharpar, the rivers of Damascus, better than all the waters of Israel?

Commentary
by Stephanie Biggs-Scribner

Could I not wash in them, and be clean?" (II Kings 5:12a) In a rage, he refuses to follow Elisha's directions, but his servants persuade him that he has nothing to lose by trying. So he goes and immerses himself seven times in the Jordan; and, after the seventh time, his flesh is "restored like the flesh of a young boy...." (II Kings 5:14)

The story is problematic in that it makes no comment about nations overpowering other nations or about forced labor and child labor. The story's purpose and the young girl's purpose are the same: to reveal Israel's God as more powerful than the gods of other nations.

When the unnamed young girl in service to the unnamed wife of Naaman learns that he has leprosy, she need not say anything. Yet, without prompting, this young girl expresses how unfortunate it is that Naaman is not with the prophet (Elisha) in Samaria. She has faith that Elisha could cure Naaman's leprosy. With horses and chariots laden with gifts, Naaman travels to find Elisha.

Elisha sends word through an intermediary that Naaman should wash himself seven times in the Jordan to be healed. When Naaman refuses to follow Elisha's directions, Naaman's servants offer their advice. We see a lesson in both the girl's offer of information and the words of the servants. They are brave enough to speak out, even though they risk being punished for offering their opinions. Bravery such as this shows that these servants, at least one of whom was "acquired" through the raiding of one culture by another, are undaunted by their situation and have not lost their sense of self-respect. The young girl's words teach Naaman where to go for help. They show that she is generous enough to have compassion on people of other traditions—even oppressors of her own people. They also show that her community has taught her well about her own tradition. (Deuteronomy 6:7)

LETTERS ON THE CAPTIVE GIRL
by Stephanie and Maggie Biggs-Scribner

Dear Maggie,

The next story is one that we can teach each other about! First, I will teach you the story about a girl who is forced to work as a slave. Then you can teach me about child labor, since you've been studying that in school.

This story is about an army commander named Naaman. Naaman and his army capture some people from Israel and make them slaves. One of the people they take is a young girl. We don't know her name or how old she was. But she does something really brave. You see, the commander who captured her, Naaman, has a skin disease. And this girl, working for Naaman's wife, speaks up about his disease! She says : "If only my lord were with the prophet who is in Samaria! He would cure him of his leprosy."

No sooner does word reach Naaman that Elisha might be able to cure him than he packs up a lot of presents and travels to Israel to visit Elisha. Elisha instructs Naaman to bathe in the Jordan River seven times and then he will be clean. Naaman gets mad! He says that the rivers in his own lands are better. But in the end, some of Naaman's servants point out that dipping down into the water seven times is easy, so he ought to try it.

The story does not say whether the young girl is one of the servants who point that out. It does not really matter. She's the one who started the whole process to get Naaman healed. Also, both times when servants recommend something to Naaman about his health, they give advice without asking if they may speak. That's a brave thing for a servant to do.

Also, when the girl speaks up in the very beginning, she calls Naaman her "lord." And when the group of servants encourages Naaman to bathe in the Jordan, they call him "father." These names were used to show respect. If his servants showed disrespect, he could have them killed.

But it is odd that the girl and the other servants use such respectful names for Naaman, yet they speak up without being given permission to talk. Plus they are giving health suggestions to a man who uses them as slaves! Maggie, please write me a letter that explains what you know about child labor today. How is it like the forced labor of the girl servant in this Bible story? Be sure to tell me if you see a connection between the Bible story and the kind of child labor you are studying in school. Okay?

Love, Mom

63

Dear Mom,

I know that child labor was probably legal when this story happened, so the girl couldn't even run away and get help. She might have been fed well and have had a good place to sleep, but as long as she had to work for someone outside her family, it was child labor.

I wonder what the girl felt like when she spoke up about Naaman's disease. She might have been treated well enough that she wanted to bring her master and mistress joy, but she also might have spoken up to earn better treatment.

Mom, I'm writing this because I studied child labor for a project at school. My country to look up was India. Child labor is a big deal there. It's not just a bunch of kids working for fun or to get money of their own. Kids who work don't necessarily want to work. They have to do it for the sake of their parents. The "inside scoop" is that most kids work to pay off debt their parents owe. In India, debt can range from 500 to 7,500 rupees. Though it sounds like a lot, 500 rupees is only $11.00 and 7,500 is about $165.00. Kids in child labor not only work long, hard hours in harsh conditions, but they don't get to go to school. Most kids don't know how to read and write. India has the most child labor of any country in the world. You can help by going to www.leapoffaith.com, www.laborrights.org, or www.stopchildlabor.org.

I hope this helps stop child labor.

Love, Maggie

A DIFFERENT VIEW: AN INVISIBLE GIRL *by Linda H. Hollies*

People like me are not paid much notice. People like me are supposed to be quiet, do our work, and not draw any attention to ourselves. People like me—young, foreign, and a servant—are seldom either seen or heard. But I made a distinct difference in the home where I worked. I saved an important man's life. If it had not been for me and my desire to help, he would have died in shame in the leper's colony, away from his family.

I come from a strong line of hardworking people. Our nation had been slaves in Egypt for years. Currently my people live in Israel, which is at war on and off with Syria. Sometimes we win, for God is on our side. Sometimes we lose because of sin among our leaders. On one war raid, I was stolen as part of the "spoils of war." I was placed in the home of Naaman, the commander of the Syrian army, as the maid to his wife. Neither one of them paid any attention to me. They couldn't care less about how I cried when my family could not find the money to ransom me. They never asked me how I felt about losing my friends and my homeland. They never asked me what I liked or didn't like. I was their slave.

The senior housekeeper told me how to do my job. The other servants didn't know and didn't care that, at home, I'd had my own maid. I missed my nanny and her daughter, who had been growing up with me, but these strange people knew nothing about it. They didn't speak my language, and they never tried to communicate with me. Since they talked all around me, I began to pick up a few words of their language. Soon I could make out their conversations, but I never said a word. I was invisible. For all they knew, I might have been dumb too. I knew how to keep my mouth closed and I tried hard to stay out of their way.

I'm not saying they were mean to me. I just didn't matter to them. I was an object to them. The only time I seemed to matter was when something was missing that the lady wanted—or something was needed by her. I didn't have a name that they knew. They never even asked me my Hebrew name. I knew how to be present when my mistress needed me. She seldom had to call me. And when she wanted something, she would never address me or look me in the eye. That might have made her realize that I, too, was human. No, she would just tell me what she wanted done and I would do it.

Of course I wasn't the only Hebrew slave in the area. We got together whenever possible and talked about all the news that we had learned during our hours of serving. That was how I heard, through the house grapevine, that Naaman had been diagnosed with leprosy. For my owners, this was not good news at all.

Leprosy is a death sentence. Leprosy is not a kind illness. And leprosy is contagious. Soon Naaman was going to be fired from his job, lose his home, lose his importance, and be forced to go and live in the leper's colony outside the walls of the town. Lepers were shunned by everyone in the town, for their body parts would fall off. They were wrapped in bloody bandages, and they had to shout out, "Unclean, unclean, unclean!" if anyone began to walk close to where they were. It didn't make any difference who you were. If you had leprosy you were banned from civilization.

Soon, Mr. High and Mighty Man of War was going to know exactly how I felt when I was taken away from my home. It wouldn't be long until the man of honor and valor would be an outcast. The time was soon approaching when he would have to leave all that was important to him and go and live among strangers, just as he made me do when he brought me to this land as a captive.

It wasn't going to be a pretty picture. And I had a secret.

I knew a man where I used to live who could perform miracles. I knew a man who was in touch with God. I knew a man who had received a double anointing of the prophet Elijah's spirit and would be able to heal Naaman. All of us from Israel knew about Elisha and the school of prophets in Israel, but it was our secret.

Why would I help the very man who had taken me away from my home? Why would I want to offer assistance to people who acted as if I didn't exist except to work for them? Why in the world would it matter to me that this family was going to be split and that their hearts would soon feel as mine had felt each and every day? I had a secret. They didn't even know my name. Would they listen to me? I was only a young girl, an invisible housekeeper, a serving maid, a slave.

When I went into her quarters one morning, I could tell that Naaman's wife had a very sad heart. I could see the tears on her face. I could tell that Naaman was not very talkative when he came home in the evenings. There was an atmosphere of grieving in the home that I could distinctly feel and identify. Still, I wanted to keep my secret. But I served the Living God.

The God we serve is filled with generous compassion. The God we serve brought us out of slavery in Egypt, and we celebrate this event each year with the Passover meal. The God we serve is a healer and a mighty deliverer, who opened the Red Sea for our ancestors. My Syrian masters had stolen my body, but they could not steal my mind. In my heart, I continued to serve the True and Living God. So I shared the secret with Naaman's wife. For the first time, she listened to me.

I was the only hope she and her husband had left. They had exhausted all of their means to no avail. When I shared the news of Elisha, the prophet of God, Naaman's wife went running to find her husband. I guess people can see and hear you when you have something to say that they want to hear. All of a sudden, I was no longer invisible. The important Naaman came home immediately to ask about where Elisha could be found. I didn't hold out on him. I told him all I knew.

Naaman tried to buy his healing with silver, gold, and fancy clothing. He was silly enough to think that riches would influence our God, but Elisha wouldn't take anything. Naaman was also silly enough to expect Elisha to act like a magician. I guess Naaman was waiting for Elisha to recite some mumbo jumbo and wave his arms to make the leprosy go away. Naaman was angry when Elisha simply told him to wash in the River Jordan seven times. It took other servants to convince Naaman that God's healing might come from simple obedience! When washing in the Jordan seven times got rid of the leprosy, it finally dawned on Naaman that our God is an awesome God!

Maybe now Naaman will take me back to where I was captured so that I can be reunited with my family! What a small price that would be to pay for having his health and his future back, and I would be ecstatic! If I'd kept my secret to myself out of spite, I could have spent the rest of my life as a slave. Now I will always have a place in Naaman's home and in his heart. I shared with Naaman's family the secret of our God. Who would have thought that an invisible and silent servant would have something worthwhile to share with her people's powerful enemies? Maybe it was because I *could* share that God let me be stolen in the first place. Who knows? Maybe tomorrow I will go home.

LETTERS ON YOUNG JESUS IN THE TEMPLE

by Stephanie and Maggie Biggs-Scribner

Dear Maggie,

The next story we should think about is the one we can piece together about Jesus as a child. Mark and John don't even mention Jesus' childhood. Luke tells of two prophets who predict great things for him when he is brought to the temple in Jerusalem as a baby to be presented to the Lord. Matthew tells a story that reminds us of the slaughter of babies in the story of Moses and says that Mary and Joseph went into Egypt to keep Jesus from being killed by Herod.

The name "Jesus" is our English way of saying a Greek name (Iēsous), and the Greek name comes from a Hebrew name. Can you guess what the Hebrew name is? It's "Joshua." Do you remember any of the stories about Joshua? When Moses led the people out of Egypt on a long journey to the Promised Land, Moses died before they could even get there. A young man named Joshua had to take over. The name "Joshua" means "God is salvation." Joshua led the people into the land of their salvation, the Promised Land. And now in the story of Jesus, a baby is born who will lead his people to salvation. The Bible is full of parallel stories like this.

The next thing we know about Jesus comes from the Gospel of Luke. Jesus is now twelve years old—just one year before a Jewish boy today goes through his Bar Mitzvah. The young Jesus goes with his family to Jerusalem to celebrate Passover. After the celebration, Mary and Joseph start to go back home to Nazareth. They walk for a whole day without Jesus, thinking he's somewhere with the rest of the crowd going home to Nazareth. When they figure out that he is missing, they go into a panic and hurry back to Jerusalem to look for him. They look for three days before they find him! Imagine their surprise when they finally find him and he's in the temple talking with the teachers there!

When they find him, Mary asks Jesus why he stayed back like that and tells him that she and Joseph were searching frantically for him. Jesus asks why they were searching for him when they should have known he would be in the temple. They all go home to Nazareth, and Jesus obeys his parents till he grows up. But Mary continues to think about what had happened. So do I. Do you?

Love, Mom

69

Dear Mom,

Yes, I do think about the story of Jesus as a child, and I think of how obvious it really is that Mary and Joseph would find him in the temple. They knew that Jesus' job was to be a teacher, and before you can teach you must learn. The only part that disturbs me is that Mary and Joseph just assumed he was going home with everyone else and never bothered to check!

I do think that seeing connections between different parts of the Bible makes the stories come alive. Knowing that Joshua had the same name as Jesus is cool!

Love, Maggie

A DIFFERENT VIEW: JESUS, A DREAMER *by Linda H. Hollies*

Although I willingly laid aside my power to create worlds so that I could grow into time within the space of a mother's womb, I had a dream. Even though I gave up my ability to speak things into existence when I took on human flesh and moved into an earthly neighborhood, still I had a dream. It made no difference that I ceased speaking the language of the heavens so that my mother could teach me to speak the words of earth. I always had a dream.

Dreams help us to prepare our movements through life. Dreams help us to be patient in confining and limiting spaces, awaiting the right time, the right moment, and the right opportunity to become more, to do more, and to make our mark on the world. Dreams counseled me to submit to my earthly father when he taught me to become a carpenter. What a fitting apprenticeship for one who was born to build lives, to help people reach their greatest potential.

I dreamed that one day I would go into the midst of those who were experts about God. I dreamed that one day I would be able to engage in conversation with those who studied, memorized, and loved the Torah. I dreamed that I could help them know, love, and understand the God of the Torah better. I had a dream that I could teach the teachers more about what they were called to teach.

It was an enriching experience to grow up in a family and learn to interact with parents and with siblings. It was right that I also submit to learning from those outside my family who had been chosen by God to be the lights of the world. I looked forward every Sabbath to hearing the rabbis teach about God. It all reminded me of the place that I longed for within the deepest recesses of my heart. Living on this earth mandated that I keep my dream.

I was born to die! Although there was a celebration at my birth, although angels sang and the heavens rejoiced over my coming into the world in a stinky stable, it was no secret to either of my parents that I was born to be the savior of our people. And I knew that I would have to do this by living fully in a short space and by dying. To have this certainty engraved in my human spirit was not the easiest reality to live with.

Our family tradition of going to worship together, singing the Psalms, hearing the Torah, and listening to the interpretations was always a tug at my soul. I realized that the rabbis were limited in their knowledge of the One who sent me. My dream was to help them have an intimate relationship with the Ancient of Days. This dream was birthed with me. It lived, burned, and followed me every day of my life.

When I was born, our country was occupied by the Romans and ruled by a king they had approved. Jews were not the favorite or most politically popular people in the world. We Jews lived together, worked together, and traveled together for protection. A great multitude of us went up to Jerusalem to celebrate Passover the year I was twelve. It was the year before my Bar Mitzvah. The dream of watching, listening, and sharing what I knew was about to come into reality.

Of course, I traveled with the boys from my village, who were kept in the middle of the adult males. We had fun talking, playing, and helping to look out for the smaller children. It was a great journey, sort of like a huge family reunion. But when we got to Jerusalem, I forgot all about the boys my own age. I only wanted to sit in the temple and listen to the rabbis debate.

It wasn't that I went to teach the rabbis anything. They were there to try to understand the Scriptures. I sat and listened to a history that I'd known from before the beginning of time. All of their conversation brought back to me glimpses of how life had been when Abba chose a people who were no people and created them into a great nation. The rabbis allowed me to listen and even to ask questions. They encouraged me to stretch, think, and grow. I was living my dream, and the time simply slipped away!

I ate and slept with the rabbis, who were cared for by temple assistants. The conversations, the debates, even the disagreements among the rabbis were thrilling. I just slipped in questions for their consideration and made comments that provoked them to talk more. When my parents burst into the temple looking afraid, I was shocked to discover that my group had left for home over three days before!

There was never any intention on my part to worry or frustrate my parents. But of all people, they knew the circumstances of my birth. My mother should have remembered what the rabbi Simeon and the prophet Anna had said about me. (Luke 2:25-38) My mother should have known that I came into the world as the Lamb of God who was to take away the sin of the world. And my earthly father should have remembered his own dream that had kept him from setting my pregnant mother aside before their marriage. (Matt. 1:18-25) My parents seemed to have forgotten that I had a mission. I could never forget!

When my parents asked me why I had made them worry by not staying with the group, I had to remind them both that I was sent to earth to serve God. These two wonderful folks were the parents God had given me. I had great love and respect for both of them. However, they both had been warned before I came into the world that I was on earth with an assignment from God. Still, God told me to submit to my earthly parents. So I went back with them to Nazareth, apologizing all the way. And the dream in me lived on!

THE BOY WHO OFFERED WHAT HE HAD

(John 6:1-15; Matthew 14:13-21; Mark 6:32-44; Luke 9:10-17)

One of the few stories recorded by all four Gospels is the feeding of the multitude. Through this story we see the reciprocal aspect of adult/child relationships. In this story it is adults who are fed—even spiritually sustained—through the actions of a youth. While the miraculous feeding occurs in all four Gospels, our study will address chiefly John's version, the only one where the boy is mentioned. In particular, we will consider the role that Passover plays in the story. The other three Gospels do not associate this event with the Passover.

John indicates that this story takes place near Passover, one of three times in the year when pilgrimages were made. The Passover pilgrimage focused on retelling the night before the journey out of Egypt, when the angel of death passed over the homes of the Hebrews, claiming the lives of firstborn Egyptian males. (Exodus 12:1-14) It also focused on the present time, during which the pilgrim travelers participated in a customary meal and celebration together, and on the future, during which descendants of the Jewish tradition could be expected to carry out the same traditions. In all of the times focused on through pilgrimage, God is understood as being present with the nation. A pilgrimage, wherein all points of time collapse into one, is a holy event. Emotional images are stirred up when the story mentions that Passover is near and a large crowd is coming toward Jesus. (John 6:5a)[36]

The overwhelming size of the crowd is underscored when Jesus and Philip converse about buying food for the people. (John 6:5-7) Philip remarks that even "six months' wages would not buy enough bread for each of them to get a little." Andrew tentatively suggests: "There is a boy here who has five barley loaves and two fish. But what are they among so many people?" (John 6:8-9)

Without hesitation, Jesus tells his disciples to make the people sit down. Mark observes that the disciples seat them in groups of hundreds and of fifties. (Mark 6:40) This makes estimating the size of the crowd easier. Each Gospel indicates that there are about 5,000 people, not counting women and children! Jesus blesses and breaks the five loaves and two fish for distribution to the crowd. The people eat as much as they want and there are still 12 baskets of leftovers. (John 6:12-13)

This story has piqued the interest of readers for years. What became of the boy who shared his food? Were his mother and father pleased or horrified when the boy gave away the food they had packed for the family? All we know is that the boy offered everything he had in faith that Jesus could use it—without being deterred by the fact that it was way too little to feed such a large crowd. Asking questions about the boy and the family involved with him is a good, thoughtful thing to do. Yet it might cause us to miss an important point: that, during the preparations for this holy pilgrimage, a young boy is the provider for the physical needs of a whole crowd of people. Even today, readers looking for spiritual inspiration are "fed" by the image of this young boy's enterprise.

Commentary
by Stephanie Biggs-Scribner

LETTERS ON THE BOY WHO OFFERED WHAT HE HAD

by Stephanie and Maggie Biggs-Scribner

Dear Maggie,

In this last story, Passover is getting close, and Passover is a pilgrimage holiday. All holidays are special and bring a lot of people together, but pilgrimages are a little different. To go on a pilgrimage, people have to travel to a special place. For Passover, the special destination is Jerusalem.

It's really neat to have special places where a huge crowd gets together for a holiday. Do you remember celebrating Passover with my friend from school back in New York? You asked the ritual questions (in German!) for my friend, head of the house, to answer."Warum ist diese Nacht so ganz anders als die übrigen Nächte?" ("Why is this night completely different from any other night?) You did very well! And you got a present for hiding and then finding the afikoman.[37] Well, that was the Passover we were celebrating, and when it was over, we all said, "Next year in Jerusalem!"

Passover in Jerusalem is the celebration that was getting ready to happen in our story. Lots of people were showing up to celebrate. Many of the pilgrims took some time to go see Jesus teach, since they'd heard about his miracles. They listened to him all day. Well, you know how people are...they get hungry!

So Jesus told his disciples to feed them. But they said not even six months of wages would buy enough to feed that many people! So one of the disciples, Andrew, said there was a boy who had brought some food. He had five loaves of barley bread and two fish. That doesn't sound like very much for a crowd that big, but somehow Jesus made it work. When he broke the loaves and the fish into pieces, around 5,000 people, not counting women and children, were fed. The disciples even gathered up twelve baskets of leftovers! The boy and the disciples and Jesus all worked together to make sure everyone got some food.

This is our last letter about children in the Bible. As in real life, these stories have people in them who are dealing with problems. And just like in real life, things go better when people work together—sort of like you and Dad and I work together to take care of your new

74

puppy, Sugar. Since she had to leave her mommy before she was really old enough, Sugar needs somebody with her all the time, so we have to take turns watching her. You get her in the afternoons, but Dad and I take care of her while you are at school or asleep. Things work best when everyone shares the work. I've enjoyed your letters, and I hope you've enjoyed reading about children in the Bible.

Love, Mom

Dear Mom,

Since I can write about anything, I'll write about what I think about having children in the Bible. I think it's a great idea, because sometimes we children know or remember something really important that comes in handy. In most of these stories, we are the ones that come in handy.

I love teamwork, because you and whoever you're working with always get more if you work together. Do you know what TEAM stands for? Together Everyone Achieves More! I love soccer partly because of my team. If I had to play soccer as a one-on-one type gig, then I would absolutely hate it.

Love,
Maggie

A DIFFERENT VIEW: A BOY AND HIS LUNCH *by Linda H. Hollies*

I had never seen so many people in my whole life. There were pilgrims everywhere. If my father had not picked me up and let me ride on his back, I might have been crushed. A huge crowd was rushing ahead, trying to get a good spot from which to hear a teacher everyone was buzzing about. I asked Dad why he and Mom were following the crowd. Dad said that we were going to hear Jesus, a dynamic, life-changing teacher. We might get to witness one of his healings—maybe even see him work a miracle. My mom and dad were really excited about getting close enough to hear him. I didn't have a choice. I was in a sea of folks moving towards the hill area.

It was hot. It was dusty. And if I could have walked with some of the other children my own age, it might have been fun. But the little ones, who walked very slowly, had to stay with the women, while I was big enough to walk with the men, though not big enough to go off by myself. I couldn't see over the men, so my father lifted me onto his back with his arms under my legs. From there I could see far up the road. Believe me, being bounced up and down while my father walked and talked with the other adult men was not fun at all. But getting squashed would have been worse.

We finally got to a place where we could see the Teacher and all the other men and women who encircled him. He was sitting up high on the hill, and we threaded through the multitude to get as close as we could. Because I was shorter than the men, I was allowed to go right up front with some of the other boys my height as long as my father could see me. He had been warned by my mother not to lose me!

I'm small for my age, but I'm almost 12. I'm preparing for my Bar Mitzvah. Soon, I will be able to recite the Shema[38] and even get to read from the Holy Scrolls in front of our village. My mom will be smiling at me. I'm her "big boy." That's what she calls me all the time. I wouldn't get lost. I'm almost an adult. Still, I tried to stay within my father's sight. I didn't want him to yell at me and embarrass me in front of my friends.

We were there all day long. Our stomachs began to growl. The crowd began to get anxious. All of us wanted to know how so many people were going to get some supper at the same time. Maybe no other family had remembered to bring food along. Mom had made a lunch for me, which I had in a sack, but what about the rest of this congregation? I didn't want to eat in front of them with everybody staring hungrily at me.

Whatever their personal reasons for coming, people had showed up in great numbers. An eyewitness reporter named Matthew said there were about five thousand men, besides women and children. Can you believe that all of us children and our mothers were not even counted? It was as if only the men mattered! If you counted all the women and the children, this huge crowd probably numbered well over fifteen thousand people. Jesus looked at the multitude and asked a man standing next to him, a disciple named Philip, "Where are we to buy bread for these people to eat?" I think he did this to see what Philip would say. I think he already had a plan.

Philip answered the way any logical person would. He said, "Six months' wages would not buy enough bread for each of them to get a little." That's when I piped up and said I had some food I could share. I was young and willing to believe in miracles, so I offered my loaves and fish to Jesus. Jesus didn't seem to hear me, but another disciple named Andrew came over to ask me what I had. He looked into my sack and then he called out to Jesus: "There is a boy here who has five barley loaves and two fish. But what are they among so many people?"

The folks who were close enough to hear my offer laughed at me. They said that I was offering a micro-lunch for the multitudes. The people mocked me for my audacity. They felt that I was really naive. But Jesus did not laugh. He beckoned me to come over and he accepted the offering from my hands. Then he had everyone sit down. The crowd was so large that he had his disciples seat them in groups of hundreds and fifties. That's how the eyewitness could count them.

Jesus held up my five little barley rolls and two fish, and when he had given thanks, he broke them and distributed them to his disciples. Then the disciples went down the aisles, passing the food in baskets row by row. When everyone had eaten, Jesus told his disciples to gather up the leftovers, and what they brought back filled 12 baskets!

A miracle had been performed through me, a little nameless boy who shared what he had. I knew that my mom had fixed only enough for our family. I could see all the hungry people around me, and I knew that I didn't have enough to feed them, yet I gave all that I had. I did not put limits on what the Teacher could do with my offering. I did not speculate on what folks would say about what I'd offered. I did not hesitate, in the face of so many, to offer what I had to share. And it was more than enough!

Adults are quick to say: "No, that won't work," "You're too young to understand," or "That's not possible." I only pray that, as I grow older, I'll never forget that what was impossible became possible because of what Jesus was able to do with my simple gift.

EPILOGUE
TEACHING CHILDREN / CHILDREN TEACHING

by Stephanie Biggs-Scribner

Educating children has always been an important part of child rearing. According to Carol Meyers, women in ancient Israel had a major role in creating social stability. In particular, women in Israel probably bore the majority of the responsibility for teaching the young. The image of wisdom as a woman (Greek *Sophia,* and Hebrew *hôkmah,* both feminine words) may be an idea that germinated from this experience.[39] But what did women teach?

Deuteronomy
Commandments to teach children Jewish traditions pervade the Hebrew Bible. Two passages in Deuteronomy are especially relevant. In Deuteronomy 6:6-7, the following words are attributed to Moses:

> Keep these words that I am commanding you today in your heart. Recite them to your children and talk about them when you are at home and when you are away, when you lie down and when you rise.

These verses are a part of the famous *Shema,* a daily Jewish prayer/confession of faith.[40] Moses is also quoted about the parental obligation of teaching children in Deuteronomy 4:9-10:

> But take care and watch yourselves closely, so as neither to forget the things that your eyes have seen nor to let them slip from your mind all the days of your life; make them known to your children and your children's children—how you once stood before the LORD your God at Horeb, when the LORD said to me, "Assemble the people

for me, and I will let them hear my words, so that they may learn to fear me as long as they live on the earth, and may teach their children so."

Both Deuteronomy 6 and Deuteronomy 4 express the need to teach children, but they concern teaching children about different things.

Deuteronomy 6 insists on the importance of teaching children *what has been taught.* In this context, what has been taught probably refers to the statutes and ordinances just attributed to Moses in chapter 5. These statutes and ordinances are Deuteronomy's parallel to the famous "Ten Commandments" found in Exodus 20:1-17. The people to whom Moses is speaking in this text learn by having their trusted leader explain God's statutes and ordinances to them. According to Deuteronomy 5:5, the people have to trust Moses' words about God's commandments, because when God tried to speak directly to them, they were afraid. As a result, they have to use the trusted teachings of Moses to create a tradition.

Chapter 4 focuses on a different type of teaching. It concerns teaching children what has been learned by *experience.* The "things that your eyes have seen" (Deut. 4:9) are invoked as traditions to be passed on, because they teach lessons in and of themselves. One of the things seen by the people was described as follows: "[Y]ou approached and stood at the foot of the mountain while the mountain was blazing up to the very heavens, shrouded in dark clouds." (Deut. 4:11) The text continues to make a profound point. The people are reminded to teach their children not just about what they saw but also about what they did not see! They "saw no form; there was only a voice." (Deut. 4:12) Since the people *did not see* God, they would have no way to *make* a god to worship. (Deut. 5:8-10)

Proverbs

Proverbs is a book of wisdom that contains example after example of the education of a "child." Harold C. Washington writes, "The purpose of the book of Proverbs is to transmit insights whereby one might learn to cope with life."[41] That it was a collection of the best wisdom of the day from many sources is evident from its numerous topics, genres, and writing styles. Early in the book, a statement is made that connects learning with the familial experience—the "father's instruction" and the "mother's teaching" (Prov. 1:8-9)—as well as with safety of the self and of others. (Prov. 1:10-19) Learning from parents and other teachers is thereby established early within this book as the way to maintain security within society. This type of learning is described as wisdom.

Much more about the way Proverbs characterizes wisdom can be said. Wisdom ensures safety. "[P]rudence will watch over you; and understanding will guard you. It will save you from the way of evil, from those who speak perversely, who forsake the paths of uprightness to walk in the ways of darkness." (Prov. 2:11-13) Wisdom is powerful. Proverbs 3:19 says, "The LORD by wisdom founded the earth." Moreover, the wisdom by which the earth was founded and through which one is saved from evil is not described as an object but rather as a *person*. Specifically, Wisdom is a woman crying out in the streets and city gates. (Prov. 1:20-21) She laments ignorance, saying: "How long, O simple ones, will you love being simple? How long will scoffers delight in their scoffing and fools hate knowledge?" (Prov. 1:22) The remedy for this state of affairs is the pursuit of wisdom and the transmission of this wisdom to one's children.

Psalm 8

The Hebrew Bible not only expresses the need for adults to teach children about truth and tradition. It also contains the humbling, awe-inspiring message that children can be our teachers. Psalm 8 is a hymn of praise written in the form of an *inclusio,* in which the beginning and the ending are the same. Verse 1 matches verse 9 exactly: "O LORD, our Sovereign, how majestic is your name in all the earth!" Sandwiched between these two tributes to God is a list of some aspects of creation that exemplify the Creator's majesty.

Of all the inspirational remarks made in this psalm about God's creation, especially important for studying children in the Bible is verse 2: "Out of the mouths of babes and infants you have founded a bulwark because of your foes, to silence the enemy and the avenger."

Scholars have debated at length as to the exact the meaning and translation of this verse, but it is evident that the psalmist places high value on the insights of children. Jesus himself was quite specific about the kinds of insights children can bring to adults.

Becoming a Child

In Matthew 18:1-7, Jesus teaches that the qualities found in a child provide the example adults are to follow. The disciples ask Jesus who is the greatest in the kingdom of heaven. Jesus places a little child in the midst of them and says: "Truly I tell you, unless you change and become like children, you will never enter the kingdom of heaven. Whoever becomes humble like this child is the greatest in the kingdom of heaven." (Matt. 18:3-4)

This teaching is so important that it appears in another version in Mark 10:13-16 and Luke 18:15-17. In the passages in Mark and Luke, where Jesus says, "Let the little children come to me; do not stop them," the disciples have been functioning the way security officials do at a modern-day celebrity event. They keep the throngs of people at a comfortable distance. They regulate who gets through to Jesus. He has to warn them to let the children through, "for it is to such as these that the kingdom of God belongs." (Mark 10:14; Luke 18:16)

In these passages, Jesus asserts that heaven belongs to those on the bottom level of the social hierarchy—children. Only adults who can learn to be like children can enter heaven. There are many possible interpretations for what Jesus meant when he said we should change and become like children. Eugene Boring suggests the following: "humble, innocent, without lust, open and trusting, spontaneous, vulnerable, dependent, allowing oneself to be given a gift without [feeling] a compulsion to 'deserve it.'"[42] But, unless we understand society's attitudes toward children in Jesus' day, we may miss the significance of Jesus' making an example of a child.

In the first century A.D., life was very difficult. Most of a community's energy was spent on mere survival. A child, who represented another mouth to feed, was valued to the extent that he or she could as soon as possible contribute to the family's survival. Thomas Aquinas, a thirteenth-century theologian, illustrated the differences between ancient family structures and those prevailing in his own time by posing the following question (still a pertinent one today): If your house was on fire and your father, mother, wife, and children were in the house, whom would you save first?[43] The answer for someone of Jesus' time would have been simple: first the father, then the mother, then the wife, and finally, if there is time, the children.

To illustrate further the ancient worldview on families and hierarchies, the word "child" in Aramaic (a commonly spoken language at the time of Jesus) is the same as the word for "servant" or "slave." For that matter, even in biblical Hebrew, slave men and women were referred to with the juvenile terms "boy" and "girl." With this background, we begin to understand the revolutionary nature of what Jesus was saying. His answer to the disciples' question about who

would be the greatest in the kingdom of heaven was that the one who was now considered the least important would be the greatest. In our era, upward mobility is valued, but Jesus was saying that if you want to be at home with him, you have to value even the most humble and unimportant members of society. In fact, you have to become humble and unimportant yourself.

If Jesus were to give the same object lesson today, he might wish to pick another group as the most humble and undervalued. In the United States, it might be street people, victims of AIDS, or people who look Middle Eastern. However, I think that the situation Jesus chose to spotlight shows us the primary importance to our churches of teaching and learning from children. Jesus showed us the value of our children as bearers of the heavenly system of values.

People in positions of power protect the power structure. Today, security and privilege depend on power. However, to be admissible into heaven, one must release all power to the Reign of God. These were hard words for the disciples to hear and are hard words for us, too! But his listeners' concept of heaven itself was changed by Jesus' use of a child to illustrate the qualities that belong in heaven.

Millstones and Our Future: Removing the Stumbling Blocks

The Gospel of Matthew, more than the other three Gospels, is interested in establishing a post-resurrection community of faith (i.e., the church). We know that within churches there are established hierarchies that determine who gets to make decisions. Children are at the bottom of the hierarchy, followed by youth. Programs are directed *at* children and youth but are rarely planned in consultation *with* them. I think the question that Jesus raises about what a child's place is in the community of faith is worthy of consideration.

Where, when, and how are our children to receive their religious education and experience?

Do we take seriously the command of Jesus to let the children come? The children no longer represent the bottom of our society as they did in Jesus' time, but how do adults treat these little ones who do not have any power or influence today?

The uncomfortable nature of teaching children religious tradition may have been part of the disciples' problem in Mark 10. Jesus had been teaching about marriage, adultery, and other difficult topics when people brought their children for him to "touch" (i.e., bless). The disciples felt that this was inappropriate and spoke sternly to those who wanted to "crash the party," so to speak. But Jesus told them to let the children come. (Mark 10:14)

Matthew 18:5 broadens the concept expressed in Mark by quoting Jesus as saying that *welcoming* a child in his name is the same as welcoming him. These are positive examples of the importance of teaching children and of learning from them. As for the consequences of not teaching them (or teaching them the wrong things), Jesus says, "If any of you put a stumbling block before one of these little ones who believe in me, it would be better for you if a great millstone were fastened around your neck and you were drowned in the depth of the sea." (Matt. 18:6) The millstone that Jesus refers to is the big one that has to be pulled by a draft animal ("donkey's millstone" is literally what the text says). Such millstones, which were used to grind large quantities of flour at the town's communal mill, would be several feet tall and weigh hundreds of pounds. May God preserve us all from becoming a stumbling block to other believers, especially children.

How does this book fit into the picture? Teaching children religious tradition is a duty of adults, but we have seen that the stories in the Bible are not always "child-friendly." One message of this book is that, if we expect our children to love studying the Scriptures as much as we do, it's important to expose them gradually to some of the tougher Bible stories as they grow mature enough to grapple with them. This is why the religious education of children must be ongoing! There are always new levels of analysis to be reached. Likewise, we ourselves must keep coming back to the stories that trouble us in search of new revelations of their meaning.

The Bible is eternally interesting because it gives us an endless variety of questions, apparent contradictions, and counterintuitive concepts to ponder and work out. We hope that the multiple approaches to Bible study presented in this book—among them scholarly interpretation (exegesis), linguistic analysis, dialogue about the stories (both spoken and through correspondence), and the creation of first-person accounts from the viewpoint of characters in the Bible stories—have suggested useful and interesting ways of studying Scripture. We also hope that the book has suggested new ways of teaching children to love studying the Bible.

ENDNOTES

1. See Richard P. Heitzenrater, who himself refers to the work of Philippe Airès. Richard P. Heitzenrater, "John Wesley and Children," 279-299, in *The Child in Christian Thought,* Marcia J. Bunge, editor (Grand Rapids, MI: William B. Eerdmans Publishing Company, 2001), 280.

2. Terence E. Fretheim, "The Book of Genesis: Introduction, Commentary and Reflections," 319-674, in *The New Interpreter's Bible,* vol. 1 (Nashville: Abingdon Press, 1994), 372.

3. Frederick W. Knoblock, "Adoption," 76-79, in vol. 1 of *The Anchor Bible Dictionary,* D. N. Freedman, editor (New York: Doubleday, 1996), 77.

4. Ellen Frankel, *The Five Books of Miriam: A Woman's Commentary on the Torah* (San Francisco, CA: HarperSanFrancisco, 1996), 17-18.

5. Renita J. Weems, *Just a Sister Away: A Womanist Vision of Women's Relationships in the Bible* (San Diego, CA: LuraMedia, 1988), 1.

6. Fretheim, "The Book of Genesis," 489.

7. *Ibid.*

8. Fretheim, 490.

9. The story of the sacrifice presumed to be Ishmael is found in Surah 37:100-106 of the Qur'an. In translation by Abdullah Yusuf Ali, the text says: "'O my GOD! Grant me a righteous [son]!' So We gave him the good news of a boy ready to suffer and forbear. Then when [the son] reached [the age of] [serious] work with him, he said: 'O my son! I see in vision that I offer you in a sacrifice; now see what is your view!' [The son] said: 'O my father! Do as you are commanded; you will find me, if Allah so wills, practicing patience and constancy!' So when they had both submitted their wills [to Allah] and had laid him prostrate on his forehead [for sacrifice], We called out to him, 'O Abraham! You have already fulfilled the vision!' Thus indeed do We reward those who do right. For this was obviously a trial." Abdullah Yusuf Ali, *The Qur'an Translation,* 3d edition (Elmhurst, NY: Tahrike Tarsile Qur'an Inc., 1998), 296.

10. Cyril Glassé, *The New Encyclopedia of Islam,* rev. ed. of *The Concise Encyclopedia of Islam* (Walnut Creek, NY: AltaMira Press, 2001), 221.

11. Weems, *Just a Sister Away,* 19.

12. Ben Affleck's work inspired by this Genesis story is "Joseph, King of Dreams," Universal City, CA: Dreamworks Home Entertainment, 2000. "Joseph and the Amazing Technicolor Dreamcoat" is a musical written by Tim Rice and Andrew Lloyd Webber. It was released on DVD at Universal City Plaza: Universal Studios, CA, 2000.

13. At this point in the story, Rachel has had such difficulty conceiving that, in order to get even with her sister, Leah, she has given Jacob her maid, Bilhah, with whom to bear a child. When Rachel finally conceives, Bilhah has borne Jacob two children. For a summary of Jacob's wives and children, see Genesis 35:22-26.

14. Fretheim observantly notes: "The wordplays on the children's names...are not really etymologies, but reflection on the familial conflict and God's actions related thereto." Fretheim, "The Book of Genesis," 554.

15. William F. Arndt and F. Wilbur Gingrich, *A Greek-English Lexicon of the New Testament and Other Early Christian Literature,* 2d English edition (Chicago: University of Chicago Press, 1979).

16. Musa W. Dube, *Postcolonial Feminist Interpretation of the Bible* (St. Louis, MO: Chalice Press, 2000), 147.

17. *Ibid.,* 154.

18. *Ibid.,* 155.

19. Walter Brueggemann, "The Book of Exodus: Introduction, Commentary, and Reflections," 675-981, in *The New Interpreter's Bible,* vol. 1 (Nashville: Abingdon Press, 1994), 699.

20. *Ibid.,* 700.

21. David Marcus, *Jephthah and His Vow* (Lubbock, TX: Texas Tech Press, 1986), 7.

22. The account of their commitments to one anoth-

er in Judges 11:8-11 has been memorialized today with matching necklaces called a *Mizpah* worn by couples. Each partner takes half of the necklace and wears it to symbolize that God holds together their relationship even when the two of them are apart.

23. This Ammonite nation that threatens the Israelite people is linked to the story of Lot's daughters' commission of incest in order to bear children. Lot's younger daughter gives birth to a son, who becomes the ancestor of the Ammonites. (Gen. 19:36-38)

24. Using stories like that of Jephthah's daughter to teach obedience to parents was commonplace for a time in Western tradition. But, in fact, a book of Bible readings for children recommending Judges 11 was published as late as 1959! It was *Bible Readings for Boys and Girls: Selected Passages from the Revised Standard Version of the Holy Bible*, Lynd Ward, illustrator (New York: Thomas Nelson & Sons, 1959), 60. And even in the year 2000, a Bible illustrated for children included the story of Jephthah's daughter in its section called "Life in Canaan." See Selina Hastings, *The Children's Illustrated Bible*, B. Alison Weir, editor; Eric Thomas and Amy Burch, illustrators, 1st American edition (New York: Dorling Kindersley Publishing, 2000), 98-99.

25. Joseph R. Jeter, Jr., "Preaching Judges," *Preaching Classic Texts* (St. Louis, MO: Chalice Press, 2003), 96.

26. The text does not actually state the number of those who were able to eat from the miraculous meal. Rather, it declares that the woman's "household" ate for many days.

27. For instance, Deuteronomy 28:53-57 describes the eating of one's own children as a punishment for not having served "the LORD your God joyfully and with gladness of heart for the abundance of everything." (Deut. 28:47) And because of their "abominations," the LORD will bring about cannibalism among the people. (Ezek. 5:9-10) Moreover, part of the devastation mourned by Lamentations involved hunger that resulted in cannibalism. (Lam. 2:20)

28. That there are *any* biblical texts which discuss such a horrifying event is troubling enough, but that there are more than one is significant. There is relatively little discussion of events such as the one addressed by this book in commentaries on the books of Kings or in scholarship that addresses topical studies in the Bible. For instance, the story of the woman receives only two sentences in *The International Bible Commentary*. See Mark O'Brien and Antony Campbell, "1-2 Kings," in *The International Bible Commentary*, William R. Farmer *et al.*, editors (Collegeville, MN: Liturgical Press, 1988), 608-643. Furthermore, neither *The Interpreter's Dictionary of the Bible* nor *The Anchor Bible Dictionary* contains an entry for the topic of "cannibalism."

29. Mordecai Cogan and Hayim Tadmor, *II Kings: A New Translation with Introduction and Commentary* (New York: Doubleday, 1988), 79.

30. Presumed to be Jehoram, last mentioned in II Kings 3:8. Many debate about which king must really have been reigning in order for these circumstances to have taken place. My concern here, however, is not with chronological exactitude but with the circumstances as they are relayed by the text. Therefore, my interest in the king concerns his anonymity. The effect of leaving him nameless is to diminish his royal authority. This is emphasized all the more when we read his rhetorical response, in effect, "From where will I get help for you?" and also when we hear that he has been wearing sackcloth all along and yet has been unable to persuade God to salvage the city.

31. The exact phrase used here occurs 27 times in the Hebrew Bible and appears to be a formulaic response to a person of lower status in need of help. As in Jonah 1:6, however, it can also be used to express shock.

32. It is provocative and curious that the bystanders do not respond with shock to the mother's story. Their silence begs readers to understand them as being sympathetic to the cannibalistic mothers. They, too, are starving.

33. Musa W. Dube, "Fifty Years of Bleeding: A Storytelling Feminist Reading of Mark 5:24-43," 50-60, in *Other Ways of Reading: African Women and the Bible*, M. W. Dube, editor (Atlanta: Society of Biblical Literature, 2001), 54.

34. *Ibid.*, 59-60.

35. Noncanonical writings generally date from the first two or three centuries A.D. Although they were considered for inclusion in the canon (the list of books selected by church authorities to be approved as Holy Scriptures), they were rejected as not being authoritative. See <http://gbgm-umc.org/umw/bible> on the Internet. For noncanonical stories about Jesus' childhood power, see English translations from Greek and Latin of the Infancy Gospel of Thomas at <http://www.earlychristianwritings.com/infancythomas.html>.

36. Notice that this reading of the significance of the Passover story does not follow the same path taken by Obery M. Hendricks, Jr. In his estimation, "Jesus replaces the Passover." Hendricks' statement forces a dichotomy onto the text that is unfortunate. Instead of presenting the Passover as an event that Jesus supplants, Jesus can be joining in with the crowd during this holy time. See Obery M. Hendricks, Jr., "John," 146-182, in *The New Oxford Annotated Bible, New Testament,* 3d edition, Michael D. Coogan *et al.,* editors (Oxford, England: Oxford University Press, 2001), 157.

37. The following information was found at <http://judaism.about.com>, which provides responses to questions about Jewish ceremonies, beliefs, and practices. "Afikoman means 'dessert' in Aramaic. At the beginning of the Seder [ceremony on the first evening of Passover], the middle of the three pieces of matzah is broken. The largest piece, called the *afikoman,* is hidden. During the Seder, the person leading the service will ask the children to bring the afikoman. The Seder can only conclude after the afikoman is eaten. At this point, the children will bargain for some reward before agreeing to return the afikoman. The afikoman serves to keep the children involved and awake during the long Seder service [during which the story of the Hebrews' liberation from a tyrannical Egyptian Pharaoh is reviewed]."

38. The Shema is the Jewish confession of faith. See note 40, below.

39. Carol Meyers, *Discovering Eve: Ancient Israelite Women in Context* (New York: Oxford University Press, 1988), 150-152. For more on this topic, see Claudia V. Camp's article "Woman Wisdom" in *Women in Scripture: A Dictionary of Named and Unnamed Women in the Hebrew Bible, the Apocryphal/Deuterocanonical Books, and the New Testament,* Carol Meyers, Toni Craven, and Ross S. Kraemer, editors (Grand Rapids, MI: William B. Eerdmans Publishing Company, 2000).

40. The verses used in the Shema are Deuteronomy 6:4-9, Deuteronomy 11:13-21, and Numbers 15:37-41.

41. Harold C. Washington, "Proverbs," in *The New Oxford Annotated Bible,* 3d ed., Michael D. Coogan *et al.,* editors (Oxford, England: Oxford University Press, 2001), Hebrew Bible, 904.

42. Eugene Boring offers these examples of common interpretations of this analogy in his commentary in *The New Interpreter's Bible.* See M. Eugene Boring, "The Gospel of Matthew: Introduction, Commentary, and Reflections," 87-505, in *The New Interpreter's Bible Commentary,* vol. viii (Nashville: Abingdon Press, 1994), 374.

43. Megan McKenna, *Not Counting Women and Children: Neglected Stories from the Bible* (Maryknoll, NY: Orbis Books, 1994), 66.

RESOURCES

A full bibliography is available on the Internet at <http://gbgm-umc.org/umw/childrenofbible>.

Works Cited

Ali, Abdullah Yusuf, *The Qur'an Translation,* 3d edition (Elmhurst, NY: Tahrike Tarsile Qur'an Inc., 1998).

Arndt, William F., and F. Wilbur Gingrich, *A Greek-English Lexicon of the New Testament and Other Early Christian Literature,* 2d English edition (Chicago: University of Chicago Press, 1979).

Boring, M. Eugene, "The Gospel of Matthew: Introduction, Commentary, and Reflections," 87-505, in *The New Interpreter's Bible Commentary,* vol. viii (Nashville: Abingdon Press, 1994).

Brueggemann, Walter, "The Book of Exodus: Introduction, Commentary, and Reflections," 675-981, in *The New Interpreter's Bible,* vol. 1 (Nashville: Abingdon Press, 1994).

Camp, Claudia V., "Woman Wisdom," in *Women in Scripture: A Dictionary of Named and Unnamed Women in the Hebrew Bible, the Apocryphal/Deuterocanonical Books, and the New Testament,* Carol Meyers, Toni Craven, and Ross S. Kraemer, editors (Grand Rapids, MI: William B. Eerdmans Publishing Company, 2000).

Cogan, Mordecai, and Hayim Tadmor, *II Kings: A New Translation with Introduction and Commentary* (New York: Doubleday, 1988).

Dube, Musa W., "Fifty Years of Bleeding: A Storytelling Feminist Reading of Mark 5:24-43," 50-60, in *Other Ways of Reading: African Women and the Bible,* M. W. Dube, editor (Atlanta: Society of Biblical Literature, 2001).

Dube, Musa W., *Postcolonial Feminist Interpretation of the Bible* (St. Louis, MO: Chalice Press, 2000).

Frankel, Ellen, *The Five Books of Miriam: A Woman's Commentary on the Torah* (San Francisco, CA: HarperSanFrancisco, 1996).

Fretheim, Terence E., "The Book of Genesis: Introduction, Commentary and Reflections," 319-674, in *The New Interpreter's Bible,* vol. 1 (Nashville: Abingdon Press, 1994).

Glassé, Cyril, *The New Encyclopedia of Islam,* rev. ed. of *The Concise Encyclopedia of Islam* (Walnut Creek, NY: AltaMira Press, 2001).

Hastings, Selina, *The Children's Illustrated Bible,* B. Alison Weir, editor; Eric Thomas and Amy Burch, illustrators, 1st American edition (New York: Dorling Kindersley Publishing, 2000).

Heitzenrater, Richard P., "John Wesley and Children," 279-299, in *The Child in Christian Thought,* Marcia J. Bunge, editor (Grand Rapids, MI: William B. Eerdmans Publishing Company, 2001).

Hendricks, Obery M., Jr., "John," 146-182, in *The New Oxford Annotated Bible, New Testament,* 3d edition, Michael D. Coogan *et al.,* editors (Oxford, England: Oxford University Press, 2001).

Jeter, Joseph R., Jr., "Preaching Judges," *Preaching Classic Texts* (St. Louis, MO: Chalice Press, 2003).

Knoblock, Frederick W., "Adoption," 76-79, in vol. 1 of *The Anchor Bible Dictionary,* D. N. Freedman, editor (New York: Doubleday, 1996).

Marcus, David, *Jephthah and His Vow* (Lubbock, TX: Texas Tech Press, 1986).

McKenna, Megan, *Not Counting Women and Children: Neglected Stories from the Bible* (Maryknoll, NY: Orbis Books, 1994).

Meyers, Carol, *Discovering Eve: Ancient Israelite Women in Context* (New York: Oxford University Press, 1988).

O'Brien, Mark, and Antony Campbell, "1-2 Kings," in *The International Bible Commentary,* William R. Farmer *et al.,* editors (Collegeville, MN: Liturgical Press, 1988).

Washington, Harold C., "Proverbs," in *The New Oxford Annotated Bible,* 3d ed., Michael D. Coogan *et al.,* editors (Oxford, England: Oxford University Press, 2001).

Weems, Renita J., *Just a Sister Away: A Womanist Vision of Women's Relationships in the Bible* (San Diego, CA: LuraMedia, 1988).

Also of Interest

Birch, Bruce C., "The First and Second Books of Samuel: Introduction, Commentary, and Reflections," 947-1383, in *The New Interpreter's Bible Commentary,* vol. 2 (Nashville: Abingdon Press, 1998).

Brueggemann, Walter, *The Message of the Psalms: A Theological Commentary* (Minneapolis, MN: Augsburg, 1984).

Craven, Toni, *The Book of Psalms,* Messages of Biblical Spirituality, vol. 6 (Collegeville, MN: Liturgical Press, 1992).

Darr, Katheryn Pfisterer, *Isaiah's Vision and the Family of God,* Literary Currents in Biblical Interpretation, Danna Nolan Fewell and David M. Gunn, editors (Louisville, KY: Westminster John Knox Press, 1994).

Dube, Musa W., "To Pray the Lord's Prayer in the Global Economic Era (Matt. 6:9-13)," 611-630, in *The Bible in Africa: Transactions, Trajectories, and Trends* (Leiden, E. J. Brill, 2001).

Fox, Everett, *Give Us a King!: Samuel, Saul, and David* (New York: Shocken Books, 1999).

Grassi, Joseph A., "Child, Children," 904-907, in vol. 1 of *The Anchor Bible Dictionary,* D. N. Freedman, editor (New York: Doubleday, 1996).

Hollies, Linda H., *Pilgrim Prayers for Grandmothers* (Cleveland, OH: Pilgrim Press/ United Church Press, 1992).

Meyers, Carol, Toni Craven, and Ross S. Kraemer, *Women in Scripture: A Dictionary of Named and Unnamed Women in the Hebrew Bible, the Apocryphal/Deuterocanonical Books, and the New Testament* (Grand Rapids, MI: William B. Eerdmans Publishing Company, 2000).

Nielsen, Kirsten, *Ruth: A Commentary,* Edward Broadbridge, translator; The Old Testament Library (Louisville, KY: Westminster John Knox Press, 1997).

Tamez, Elsa, *The Scandalous Message of James: Faith without Works Is Dead* (New York: Crossroads Publishing, 2002).

The Woman's Bible Commentary, Carol A. Newsom and Sharon H. Ringe, editors (Louisville, KY: Westmister John Knox Press, 1992).

CHILDREN
OF THE
BIBLE

STUDY GUIDE

By Minerva G. Carcaño

Preparing to Teach

Create a classroom environment that captures both the amazing spirit and the difficult plight of children in biblical times and in today's world. If a child came to your class, would that child feel comfortable in the environment that you have created? Would children find your classroom inviting and hospitable? Would children be able to relate to the materials about them that you have displayed? Remember that all children look for others who look like them. Though you are teaching a class for adults, immersion in a subject often helps people learn more effectively. So immerse the participants in your class in a manner that helps them enter the world of a child.

Ask the class members to read the Prologue and Part I of the study book and to bring their Bibles to every session.

Line up all your photocopies and audiovisuals.

For photos of children, go to: http://www.children.gov.za/CoolStuff/Photo Album.htm. *(To print these photos for noncommercial use, go to:* <http://www.gov.za/terms.htm>.*)*

For a photo of the Surgeon General with a cluster of children at a daycare center, go to: <profiles.nlm.nih.gov/NN/B/D/B/M/>.

At <http://www.nlm.nih.gov/copyright.html>, *type "children photos" in the "search" box and click to access a list of diverse images.*

For a poster of a missing child, go to http://www.childwatch.org/.

SESSION 1

PROLOGUE & PART I:

CHILDREN IN TROUBLED FAMILIES

Leader: Together we will explore the stories of *Children of the Bible* and children today. You will need to consult your Bible and to draw on your experience with children. You will need to think and feel deeply as we take in the research, the mother-daughter letters, and the "Different Voices" (the stories told from the perspective of a young person in the Bible story). We will travel across the barriers of time and age to hear some children of ancient days and to compare them with children we know about today.

There is perhaps no more significant population in helping us to gauge the health and well-being of our global society than the children of the world. Children who are healthy, contented, happily curious, and excited to be alive generally reflect the quality of life of their communities.

Unfortunately, not every child has access to the resources and support systems necessary for a secure and fruitful life. As in many of the Bible stories about children, too much of the reporting on today's children is about the violence that is inflicted upon them. Violence only serves to destroy the spirit of children, and spirited children have much to teach us.

The children of the world today will determine the direction human society will take in the years to come. Thus, how we nurture and care for children today plants the seeds for the future of humanity and all the earth. The children are, even now, a life sign of years to come.

As you begin this study, gather the children into your thinking. Make them welcome in your hearts and minds. Be attentive to the care God gives to children. Seek to know the heart of Jesus, who always invites the children to come to him.

Opening Reflection

Song: "Jesus Loves the Little Children"
Jesus loves the little children,
All the children of the world.
Red and yellow, black and white,
They are precious in his sight.
Jesus loves the little children of the world.

Have three sheets of newsprint, each divided into two columns. Write one heading above the columns on each sheet: Babies, Children, Youth. Have one participant with a marker stand by each sheet. Ask class participants to call out the names of children in the Bible or the titles of their stories. Designate on which age list each belongs and write their names or story titles in column one.

When the lists seem complete, have the group come up with one or two words that describe each name or story. Alternate between the three lists so that scribes have time to write these words in column two. Post one of the following expressions of gratitude by each of the three lists.

"Thank you, God!"
"Gracias a Dios!
"Kam-sa-ham-nee-dah, Ha-na-neem!"

As the scribes write each item, lead the whole group to respond by saying "Thank you, God" in English, Spanish, or Korean, depending on which language is posted by the list.

Hymn: "Tell Me the Stories of Jesus," #277 in *The United Methodist Hymnal,* verse 2

First let me hear how the children stood round his knee,
And I shall fancy his blessing resting on me;
Words full of kindness, deeds full of grace,
All in the lovelight of Jesus' face.

(Words by William H. Parker, 1885)

Exercise: Introductions and Reading Between the Lines

- Circle the names of the children whose ages are not in doubt.
- Check off the children whose names are given.
- Put a star by any child in the Bible whom someone in the class had never heard of.
- Add any final names that come to mind.

Leader: We see from our lists that the ages of children or youth in the Bible are not always clear. We do not always have their names, nor do we have all the details that might interest us. Still, we find the stories compelling.

To introduce yourself, please select a child from the Bible with whom you relate.

Ask participants to introduce themselves to one another, in a small group or in the class as a whole, by talking about what they do or do not have in common with the child they have chosen. Allow time for introductions.

Leader: Now sit for a minute and think about what you do not know about the child or youth you have selected. On a piece of paper, make a list of things you might like to learn about the young person you have chosen.

Allow time for writing.

During this study, you might use Stephanie Biggs-Scribner's research approach to learn more about your child. Or, you might use a first-person account like those by Linda Hollies. Or, you might write a letter to a young person—or to your own "inner child"—to explore who this child of the Bible is.

Overview of Study

Leader: The lists we made as part of our opening reflection may help us uncover the themes of our study.

List the chapter titles in the study book.

In the Introduction, we see that there are several ways we can approach this book. We can read all the analysis by Stephanie, the imaginative stories by Linda, or the letters between Stephanie and her daughter, Maggie. As you read, keep your Bibles handy so that you can compare the Bible stories with the material in the study book. Insights are always waiting for us as we study the Bible.

Exercise: Troubled Children
A Historical-Anthropological Approach

Leader: Scripture allows us to see that, from the beginning of history, children have been affected by troubled families. Many times children's lives are threatened by decisions made by others around them. Children throughout the generations, however, have also brought to bear their own wisdom, compassion, innocence, and enterprising ideas.

Cain and Abel, Ishmael and Isaac, the young Joseph, and the Canaanite woman's daughter are children who suffered because they found themselves in troubled families. Sibling rivalry, family violence, slavery, homelessness, parental favoritism, being an outsider, and being part of a minority group are some of the "troubles" that disturbed and distressed the children in our study book.

The world has changed over the centuries. While human advancements have made it possible for many to have greater comforts in life, live longer, and experience more fully the beauty and gifts of God's creation, we have yet to overcome the sins that lead to the troubles our children are forced to face even today. But just as the nature of trouble has not changed that much, ancient Bible stories can still provide us with rich insights into how we are to care for all God's children.

Small Group Work

Divide the class into four smaller groups. Assign to each small group one of the stories found in Part I of the study book. Ask the small groups to be biblical anthropologists as they study the Bible story they are assigned. An anthropological approach examines customs, religious beliefs, and practices related to social class, gender, age, and ethnicity, as well as geopolitical and socioeconomic realities and other relationships between people and society. List these items on newsprint, a chalkboard, or a handout sheet.

Leader: Look at the list of items studied by biblical anthropologists. What information related to these topics can you glean from the Scripture related to your story?

At some moment in your small group, suspend conversation and spend a few minutes listing on a piece of paper or newsprint some anthropological elements of your individual lives. Take turns sharing one element that is similar to those in biblical times and one that is dissimilar.

How do the background facts provided by Stephanie and the interpretations by Linda illuminate today's anthropology? How do they illuminate ancient anthropology?

Read Stephanie and Maggie's letters for your story. Think about the anthropology of ancient times and today within the letters. What do you discover?

Have the groups share some of their insights from their anthropological work.

Exercise: Mime the Stories

Invite each group to prepare a brief mimed interpretation of its story for the whole class. Go from one story to the next in total silence. When finished, have people sit and reflect in writing on the lives of the children in these troubled families. Reflection could take the form of a prayer, a psalm, a mock news report, a prophetic cry for justice, or a simple lament.

Closing

Lead the whole class into a time of silent meditation. You may want to play soft children's music in the background as you invite the participants to lift up children to God's care in prayer. Conclude this session by inviting the participants to read in unison the prayer below.

Prayer: With the child Samuel, we say to the Lord: "Speak, for your servant is listening."

Speak to us of what we are to do to care for the children you have given us. We remember Jephthah's young daughter, slaughtered to save her father's pride. Forgive our pridefulness and give us wisdom so that the day may come when children are no longer sacrificed to pride, jealousy, arrogance, ignorance, violence, racism, sexism, consumerism, globalization, or any other false god of our making. Give us, O God, the very wisdom of Jesus, who even as a child knew that abiding in your ways alone brings wholeness and abundance of life. Amen.

(Prayer based on I Samuel 3:10b, Judges 10-11, Luke 2:41-52)

(An alternative option to the closing prayer might be to have three or four participants read their written reflections aloud. Others can be posted if people would like to share them. Provide a poster board and glue stick.)

Preparation for the Next Session

Select three participants to serve as readers for the Litany of Remembrance.

Select five participants to prepare a presentation of Marian Wright Edelman's "Children in America: A Report Card." (See pp. 94-95 below.)

Ask all participants to read Part 2 of the study book: "Children under Threat."

Prepare the classroom with the symbols of baptism—a bowl of water and a towel. You may want to add large seashells, as they are sometimes used to pour the waters of baptism on those being baptized. Pictures of the Nile River would further contribute to the participants' ability to visualize the ancient story of Moses.

Arrange for newsprint, markers, glue sticks, magazines, and other materials with which to make drawings and/or collages. Buy several rolls of pennies (or collect them from around your home). Buy inexpensive wooden skewers, small paper plates, and string to make scales.

SESSION 2
CHILDREN UNDER THREAT

Leader: In this session we will visit the Nile River with the baby Moses. As an infant, Moses was living under tremendous threat. The mighty Nile flowed through the desert as a sign of the strength of the Egyptian oppressors, yet it was along the banks of this river that the baby Moses was saved.

Through the story of the baby Moses, the waters of this great river come to remind us of the waters of our baptism. As an outward and visible sign of God's grace, the sacrament of baptism extends to all the possibility of abundant life in the fellowship of Christ's Holy Church. And as for children, our United Methodist covenant of holy baptism clearly expresses that Christ himself "has given to little children a place among the people of God, which holy privilege must not be denied them."

Every time we gather to participate in the baptism of a child, we pledge to care for the child by being the incarnation of Christ's love and to guide the child in the knowledge of God. Caring for children is a way for us, as people of God, to demonstrate our own faith and commitment to the Giver of Life.

As United Methodists, we do not believe in re-baptism, for we know baptism to be the action of the Holy Spirit. What the Holy Spirit accomplishes in our lives through baptism is done in God's own perfect way the first time and does not need to be repeated in order for God's work to be made complete. It is important, though, to remember our baptism.

During this session, lead the participants to remember their baptism and the commitments they now make as faithful Christians every time a child is baptized in their presence.

Opening Reflection

A Litany of Remembrance (4 Readers)

Read this litany with emotion and movement so that the Bible stories are recounted with passion and drama. In the part of the litany that invites participants to remember their baptism, lift the water with a shell or other cup from the bowl symbolizing baptism and allow it to flow back into the bowl. You may sprinkle it on the participants, or pass the bowl so that everyone can feel the water, or have people come to the front to dip their fingers. You might have the bowl on a table in the center of the room and have people come to it whenever they choose. The cool touch of the water engages our bodies in the act of remembrance.

Leader: One day the waters of the mighty Nile River received the baby Moses. Can you hear the breaking of the reeds as his mother, Jochebed, places him in a tiny ark of a basket and leaves him along the bank of the river in an effort to save his life? Can you hear the pounding of that mother's heart as she lets go of her beloved child? Moses' mother was a brave woman who was a model of courage and keen wisdom for her daughter Miriam, Moses' sister. Through her

care for Moses, Jochebed cared for an entire nation of God's people.

Reader 1: It is in the waters of the Nile that the baby Moses is saved, as Pharaoh's own daughter sees him, recognizes him as a Hebrew child, and yet chooses to protect this child even in defiance of her father's own edict that all the male Hebrew children should be destroyed at birth. He is named not by his birth mother but by Pharaoh's daughter, his adoptive mother, who calls him "Moses" (one drawn out of the water). With the midwives Shiphrah and Puah, Moses' birth mother Jochebed and his adoptive mother join in demonstrating what can happen when women decide to protect children from danger.

Song: "Wash, O God, Our Sons and Daughters," #605 in *The United Methodist Hymnal*, verse 1

Reader 2: Jephthah's daughter, whose story we find in the 11th chapter of Judges, and the son cannibalized in II Kings 6:24-33 did not have mothers with the courage or the wisdom of the women who surrounded the baby Moses. We know nothing of the mother of Jephthah's daughter, though we do know that the mother of Jephthah himself was a prostitute. The mothers of II Kings were desperate and hopeless women living in a time of national chaos. How different the lives of their children might have been if these women, like the women who surrounded the baby Moses, had been able to collaborate in saving the children.

Reader 3: But collaboration that saves rather than destroys takes faith in a source of power higher than human power. It takes a vision of what's possible in this life and a vision of what's possible even beyond this life.

Reader 4: At the baptism of our children, we pledge to love them and lead them in God's righteousness. In baptism, we remember that God loves all the children of the world and desires their salvation.

Song: "Wash, O God, Our Sons and Daughters," #605 in *The United Methodist Hymnal,* verse 2

Leader: Let us remember our baptism, and the baptism of our children, grateful that we depend on God's own faithful power as we care for the children.

Have everyone in some way touch or be touched by the water in the bowl.

All: We remember our baptism with gladness. We remember our pledge to God's children at their baptism and pray for faith sufficient to fulfill our pledge. And we also remember that we are called to care for all God's children. God's children include Muslim, Buddhist, Jewish, Christian, and Hindu children, as well as every other child.

Song: "Wash, O God, Our Sons and Daughters," #605 in *The United Methodist Hymnal,* verse 3

Leader: May we remember that, as we seek to care for the children, God is with us.

All: Amen!

Exercise: A Letter to Maggie

Leader: Biblical scholar Walter Brueggemann interprets the story of Moses' birth and his mother's action to save him as one that is much larger than that of one mother and one child. Brueggemann is convinced that it is truly a story of God's plan to save an entire people. Through Moses, God forms the Hebrew people and sets the stage for the salvation of all humanity. Maggie, in her letter to her mother, grasps Brueggemann's understanding of Scripture quite well when she asks:

> "Like, what if Moses had been killed? What would have happened to the Hebrews? And would there be a Bible, or would anyone even know there is a God?"

Maggie's deep-felt concerns lead us to wonder whether the children of our families and local communities, as well as children all around the globe, know that there is a God who loves them and stands with them. Have we grasped wise Maggie's insight that the baby Moses teaches Pharaoh's daughter and all of us to "be considerate to all children, not just the royal ones"?

Read Maggie's responses to all the stories of "Children under Threat." Write a brief letter of response to Maggie that addresses her concerns and your own about one or all of the stories.

Exercise: Hanging in the Balance— The Value of Children

Assign the following three stories to three small groups: Jephthah's Daughter (Judges 11), the Widow's Son (I Kings 17), and the Deal-Making Mothers (II Kings 6). Have participants create a makeshift scale of justice using two small paper plates, a wooden skewer, and string to hang the plates from opposite ends of the skewer. Hang the scale from a string so that it is balanced. Take turns holding the scale if one person gets tired. Just for fun, you may want to blindfold the person holding the scale if the person is willing.

Leader: As a group, first determine the ethical conundrum related to the child in the story. Then discuss pros and cons of the ethical decision. Put a penny in one pan of the scale or the other for each pro or con. If an element seems especially important, add more than one penny.

You could do this from the perspective of different characters in the story—or from the perspective of an unnamed person who seems missing from the story, such as the mother of Jephthah's daughter.

When you have processed the story in a small group, share any insights about points of conflict and agreement in your small group. Were there any power plays within the group? With whom did you identify in the story?

Exercise: Children Where We Live

Leader: Hear these words:

"As I look around the community where I live, read the newspaper every morning, and listen to the evening news, it is clear to me that children everywhere today live under threatening circumstances. And if the children are threatened, is not the very future of humanity under threat?"
—*Bishop Minerva Carcaño*

Ask the class participants to take a moment and consider how well children are being cared for today. Organize the participants in small groups and invite them to make an assessment of how well children are being cared for, starting from the local perspective and moving to the global one. Using your coins again, make a stack of coins for the advantages children have in your community and a stack of coins for the disadvantages. Here are some questions that can be used to guide the small groups in their assessments:

How does your local community care for its children?

What are some signs that the children in your local community are well cared for?

Are there any children left out of your community's care? Who are they?

Why are they being forgotten?

Exercise: Images of Children's Realities

Provide art materials such as newsprint, markers, construction paper, magazines from which pictures can be cut, and glue. Invite small groups to prepare collages and drawings that represent their assessments of how well children are being cared for locally and around the world.

Take time to have the small groups present their collages and discuss them. Post the collages around the room and then invite the readers selected at the end of the last session to read Marian Wright Edelman's own assessment of how the United States is doing in the care of its children.

Leader: Marian Wright Edelman, founder of the Children's Defense Fund, has been a mentor to the world on the care of children. After many years of hard work in defending the rights of children and advocating for their needs in the United States, she stopped and evaluated how this country was faring in its care for children. Using a grading system from A to F, she gave America the following report card.

Children in America: A Report Card
(5 Readers)

Leader: Since 1973, when the Children's Defense Fund began, some things have changed for the better, but other situations have become more critical. Here's how Marian Wright Edelman would evaluate our progress in five key areas.

Reader 1: *Education, Grade B*
More of our children than ever are graduating from high school and attending college. In 1973, 80% of our young people graduated from high school; in 2000, 88% graduated. The number of high school graduates attending college increased 30% in the same period. High school dropout rates went from 14% to 11%. Still, there is much to be done.

Reader 2: *Poverty, Grade D*
In 1973, the child poverty rate was 14%; by 2002, it was 17%. Among children younger than three

years old, one in six was poor in 1973; today, one in five children lives in poverty in the critical early years. Among industrialized nations, the United States ranked next to last in a 2000 UNICEF report.

Reader 3: *Teen Pregnancy, Grade C*
In 1973, there were 59 births per 1000 females aged 15-19; in 2001, that rate dropped to 45 births per 1000 females. Despite the decline, we still have the highest rate of teen births of any industrialized nation.

Reader 4: *Infant Mortality, Grade C*
Although infant mortality rates have improved since 1973 from more than 17 deaths per 1000 births to fewer than 7 per 1000, according to the US government, we are now 28th among industrialized nations (far behind France and Germany, for example).

Reader 5: *Gun Violence, Grade C*
Child gun deaths dropped by nearly 50%, but an average of eight children or teenagers are killed by firearms each day. A child in the United States is 12 times more likely to die from gunfire than a child in any other industrialized country.

(Adapted from Marian Wright Edelman, "Children in America: A Report Card," *Parade Magazine,* October 19, 2003, page 13.)

Leader: Compare the small groups' collages on the care of children with Marian Wright Edelman's Report Card. Were there any surprises? More importantly, how can women work together to improve the world's care of its children?

Give the following assignment to the small groups.

The Bible stories of Jephthah's daughter and the deal-making mothers of II Kings 6 challenge us to make our own ethical decisions. Given the realities in each story, develop a cooperative plan for how women of faith could have addressed the issues of that moment. Develop a plan and strategy that would be an alternative to child sacrifice. Try to take into consideration the historical context of the Bible story, but be bold in your plan! Take your inspiration from the women who surrounded the baby Moses and saved him for greatness.

After the small groups have had sufficient time to develop their plans, invite them to share them with the whole class. When the small groups have completed their presentations, discuss how some of the plans could be used to address the plight of children today. Invite the class to come up with additional innovative ideas.

Exercise: Risks of the Privileged— Jairus's Daughter

In small groups, examine the issues of both privilege and marginalization in the story of Jairus's daughter. Use your anthropological skills to identify the safety and danger factors in this story. After brief table-group discussions, call out your lists of safety and danger factors in the story. Jairus and his wife were affected by these factors, too. With the whole class, use a scale and pennies to weigh the risks and privileges of the daughter's life.

Exercise: Telling the Stories of Great Children

Leader: Write a brief story about a child you know who you think will become a great leader. What are this child's highest risks? What are this child's privileges conferred by social status? What are three characteristics of this child that might make her or him a great leader? Share this story with one other person in your group. Consider telling this story to the child. What are the pros and cons of doing so? What would you like to tell this child about the study on *Children of the Bible?*

Closing Meditation

Conclude with the following declaration on children's rights.

Leader: We declare that children, once considered the property of their parents, are full human beings in their own right.

People: We adults and society in general have special obligations to the children of the world.

Leader: Thus, we support the development of school systems and innovative methods of education designed to assist every child toward complete fulfillment as an individual of worth.

People: All children have the right to a high-quality education.

Leader: Children have the same rights to food, shelter, clothing, health care, and emotional well-being as adults do.

People: And these rights we affirm to be theirs, regardless of the actions or inactions of their parents or guardians.

Leader: Children must be protected from economic, physical, emotional, and sexual abuse.

People: May we dare to care for the children of the world so that they may know the love of God and lead us in building God's reign among us.

Leader: May the Holy Spirit who hovered over the waters of the Nile and protected the baby Moses, who blessed us at our baptism, and who accompanies us with the fullness of God's power help us to be bold as we care for all God's children.

People: Amen and Amen!

(Adapted from the Social Principles of The United Methodist Church, Paragraph 162.C)

Preparation for the Next Session

Recruit three volunteers to prepare and present the drama "Herod's Hit Man." You will need a person to narrate the drama, a person to play the character named Mrs. Alexander, and another to play Nilla. Invite all the participants to prepare a one-page report that describes the contemporary life of a child of a race, culture, or country other than their own. They may prepare this paper from their own experience or by using written resources, such as books or Internet articles about other cultures and countries. They may also consider interviewing people who may have knowledge about the children they have selected to write about.

Prepare a large poster board or long strip of newsprint. On it, you will invite the class to help document the many places where Nilla's hit man appears in the lives of children. Be creative. You may want to imagine what Nilla's hit man looked like and paint him onto the poster board or newsprint. Avoid racial stereotypes of criminals. Have multicolored markers ready to complete a hit-man poster.

Bring Middle Eastern as well as classical and contemporary Christian music to play during the next session. Set up the equipment needed to play it. A time of "dreaming" is recommended for the next session, with scented candles to help involve the senses. Check with participants to make sure no one has allergies to scented candles. Obtain hymnals containing the song "Tell Me the Stories of Jesus" (#277, The United Methodist Hymnal) or prepare copies of the song.

Ask the class to read Part 3 of the study book carefully and prayerfully.

SESSION 3
CHILDREN WHO SHOW ENTERPRISE

Leader: Throughout the generations, children have not only been recipients of the good and bad of the world but have also been contributors to life. Consider David, who defeated Goliath and helped the Israelites prevail over the Philistines; Joan of Arc, who led the French to freedom from the English; and Anne Frank, who, through her poignant journaling, sensitized all the world to the human brutality of the Holocaust and brought hope that such an atrocity will never again occur. These and other children have made important contributions to society through their enterprising spirit that continues to impact our lives.

In this session we will see how children of the Bible show their own enterprising spirit even in situations that seem to harbor only destruction, defeat, and even death. Through their compassionate hearts, they dream dreams of what may be possible, while adults have consigned their dreams to the realm of the impossible. Children who have not become jaded by defeat are often agents of God's transforming grace. Prepare to be amazed and inspired!

Leader: Isaiah promised the people of Israel that a savior would be coming. No one expected it would be someone like Jesus. And when Jesus told them amazing things, such as that you could move a mountain by faith or that you should become like a child to get into the kingdom of God, some scoffed. Others who loved Jesus wondered at these teachings. All along the way—even from his birth—some tried to silence Jesus' voice that spoke of love, justice, and truth.

Hymn: "Todo la Tierra," #210 in *The United Methodist Hymnal,* verse 1. Or, "O Come, O Come, Emmanuel," #211 in *The United Methodist Hymnal,* verse 1

Scripture Reading: Matthew 18:1-6 and Matthew 2:13-18

Hymn: "Away in a Manger," #217 in *The United Methodist Hymnal,* verse 1

Exercise: Herod's Hit Man (3 Readers)

Narrator: The year Nilla was in sixth grade, she and her parents decided that it would be a good thing for her to be in the church Christmas pageant being organized by the new pastor's wife. Being sensitive enough to avoid leaving anyone out or casting people in roles they didn't want to play, the pastor's wife was determined to allow the children to choose their own parts. She assigned Mary and Joseph to two older children. Then she gathered all the others and began slowly to read the familiar story of Jesus' birth. As she read, the children called out the characters they wanted to play. Angels, shepherds, kings, lambs, donkeys, camels—all claimed their roles. At the end of the story, Nilla hadn't found a role to suit her.

Mrs. Alexander, the costume manager, tried to coax Nilla into being a king or a shepherd, to no avail. Nilla finally asked if she could have the Bible. She took it off to read by herself. For 15 or 20 minutes she was hardly noticed, reading intently. After a while, she returned.

Nilla: Mrs. Alexander, I've found my role.

Mrs. Alexander: Yes, Nilla? Who are you going to be?

Nilla: A hit man.

Narrator: Mrs. Alexander swallowed hard, noticing the upward glance of the minister's wife.

Mrs. Alexander: There are no hit men in this story, honey.

Nilla: Right here, in Matthew 2, it says: "Get up, take the child and his mother, and flee to Egypt, and remain there until I tell you; for Herod is about to search for the child, to destroy him." I want to play Herod's hit man.

Mrs. Alexander: What would a hit man wear?

Nilla: All black—to hide—and he'd carry a sword.

Mrs. Alexander: You're sure that's what you want?

Nilla: Yes, ma'am.

Mrs. Alexander: Okay, Nilla. That's you.

Narrator: On that Christmas Eve, thanks to Mrs. Alexander and Nilla, their United Methodist church saw and heard a fuller version of the story of Christ's birth, with both the wonder and the horror intact. In this church, the wise men traveled to King Herod before they arrived in Bethlehem. They were accompanied by a shadowy figure on their way to the stable. Outside the stable, a hit man lurked as Mary cherished the baby and angels sang. On that Christmas Eve, Nilla's church may have been the only one in Christendom to remember Christ's birth in this more complete narrative, including not only the beauty and glory but also the fear, the evil, the grief, and the hit man.

(As recounted in Patricia H. Davis, *Beyond Nice: The Spiritual Wisdom of Adolescent Girls,* Minneapolis: Fortress, 2001, pp. 46-47; adapted)

Leader: In small groups, read Matthew 2:1-18. Look for the hit man and identify every situation in the story where you see him. Consider the child's hymn "Away in a Manger" (#217 in *The United Methodist Hymnal).* Is there danger lurking behind the gentle tune?

Exercise: Children's Realities

Ask the participants to take out the one-page reports on children of other races, cultures, or countries that they have prepared. Using Nilla's approach, ask them to take a moment to identify the hit men in the lives of the children they are reporting on. Then invite the class members to turn to two or three people around them and share their reports with one another, telling where they have found the hit man lurking in the lives of the children they wrote about.

Invite the small discussion groups to move to the hit-man poster (or newsprint) and document some of what they have learned about children, including the ways the hit man appears in the lives of the children they researched. After all the groups contribute to the hit-man poster, invite members of each group to share what they have been able to see through Nilla's eyes as they considered children's lives.

Leader: Children's eyes see the world with freshness and excitement. We learn from Nilla that, even in their innocence, they still see present danger. When allowed to be children, however, they tend to see possibilities that we adults have long ago set aside as silly or naïve. Jesus was born into a world that gave little attention to children. Some of the Bible stories that we have been studying speak to us of the cruel, unchecked violence that may be inflicted upon children. Jesus' own infancy is marked by Herod's conspiracy to kill all the infants and toddlers in and around Bethlehem who might grow up to be king of the Jews.

Exercise: Dream of the Reign of God

Even as a child, Jesus must have had a heart filled with extraordinary dreams—so much so that, at the tender age of 12, he stayed behind at the temple in Jerusalem after a Passover visit to the city to visit with the rabbis.

Four days later, Mary and Joseph found him in the temple "sitting among the teachers, listening to them and asking them questions" (Luke 2:46). Mary reprimanded Jesus for having stayed behind and caused her and Joseph to worry, but Jesus reminded her that "I must be in my Father's house" (formerly translated as "I must be about my Father's business"). Imagine that—Jesus began his ministry at the age of 12! While he didn't begin his ministry of teaching and healing until later, it appears that Jesus began his ministry of dreaming the reign of God when he studied the Scriptures with the teachers at the temple.

Invite the class to enter into a time of dreaming with Jesus as a child. Dim the lights and light scented candles. Play Middle Eastern music, as well as classical and contemporary Christian music, to set the mood of being with Jesus as a child. Encourage participants to find a comfortable space for themselves and meditate on the faith Jesus has kindled in our hearts. Ask participants to dream with Jesus the dream of the reign of God. Ask them:

What does it look like?

What changes does it bring?

What does the reign of God promise for children?

When a good length of time has been allowed for dreaming, invite the participants to share the images of the reign of God that dreaming with Jesus has brought to their minds and hearts. After each sharing, lead the group in the popular kid's response when something good is about to happen: "Yes!"

Close with the song "Heaven" from Global Praise 2. *The lyrics were composed from ideas about heaven expressed by children.*

Exercise: Seeking Inspiration from Children's Strategies

Leader: Jesus teaches us about the world as it could be if we only believed and followed in the ways of God with the faith of children. Children all around us can teach us about life, and even about what is possible with a little faith and love. Our study asks us to consider the story of the captive girl of II Kings 5, who led her master to his healing, and the Gospel story of the boy who offered what he had so that the multitude could be fed. Maggie's letters remind us that children are still held captive as economic slaves and that children and their audacious spirit "come in handy."

Divide the class into four small groups, assigning two the story of the captive girl of II Kings 5 and the other two the story of the boy who offered the fish and loaves that fed the multitude. The assignment for these small groups is twofold. First, they are to see what they can learn about helping others from the child in their assigned story. Second, they are to apply what they learned to two parallel contemporary situations: the AIDS epidemic and world hunger. The two groups studying the story of the captive girl are to prepare a plan for addressing the suffering of children who are afflicted or orphaned by AIDS, while the two groups studying the story of the boy who helped feed the multitude are to develop a plan for addressing world hunger and its impact on children. Have the small groups present their child-inspired plans to the class and discuss them.

Closing

Song: "Do, Lord, Remember Me"
Do Lord, oh do Lord, oh do remember me. (Repeat three times.)
Look away beyond the blue.
I want to be a child of God and share the gift of food. (Repeat three times.)
Look away beyond the blue.
I want be a child of God and heal my enemy. (Repeat three times.)
Look away beyond the blue.
I want to speak out like a child who holds onto the dream. (Repeat three times.)
Look away beyond the blue.

Jazz midi accompaniment is available at http://members.tripod.com/~rosemck1/jukebox-gospel.html.

Leader: Then little children were being brought to him in order that he might lay his hands on them and pray.

People: The disciples spoke sternly to those who brought them.

Leader: But Jesus said, "Let the little children come to me, and do not stop them...

People: For it is to such as these that the kingdom of God belongs."

(Based on Mark 10:13-16; Luke 18:15-17)

Closing Song: "Tell Me the Stories of Jesus," #277 in *The United Methodist Hymnal,* verse 1

Blessing: May we be like children and one day inherit the kingdom of God with them.

Preparation for the Next Session

Ask participants to read the Epilogue.

    Find materials and objects to prepare a Sunday school class for children. You may want to incorporate some of the things you have used to prepare the room for the other sessions as you bring closure to your time of teaching.

    Select psalms for singing. looking especially for sung psalms that appeal to children.

    If possible, recruit four or five children of varying ages to serve on a Child Experts Panel. Ask them to prepare for the panel by answering the question: "What can the church do to help you learn about God better?" If it is not possible to have children be present for your session, interview children and video- or audiotape your interviews with them so that you can play these tapes at the next session.

    To order the five-minute "Children of Hope" video from the Service Center, call: 800-305-9857.

SESSION 4

TEACHING CHILDREN/ CHILDREN TEACHING

Opening Reflection

Hymn: "Jesus Loves the Little Children," p. 89.

Bible Reading: Matthew 15:29-39 and John 6:1-13

Leader: In your small groups, work on the question: "Where do children appear and disappear in these scriptural passages?"

Song: "There Was a Boy" (sung to the tune of "Old MacDonald Had a Farm," with or without repetitions)

Midi accompaniment is available at: http://www.niehs.nih.gov/kids/lyrics/mcdonald.htm.

There was a crowd out on a hill
Listening to God's Word.
And on that hill there was a boy
Listening to God's Word.
With a big crowd here
And a small boy there,
Here a crowd, there a boy,
Everywhere were people
Gathered close out on a hill
Listening to God's Word.

The day was fine and people learned
How to live God's Word.
For on that hill Christ Jesus taught
How to live God's Word.
With a parable here

And a Scripture there,
Here a word, there a tale,
Everywhere a lesson.
Jesus taught and people learned
How to live God's Word.

And on that hill the day went by
Listening to God's Word.
And no one had a bite to eat
Listening to God's Word.
So the stomachs growled,
The disciples scowled,
Here a growl, there a scowl,
Everyone was hungry.
On that hill the day'd gone by
Listening to God's Word

When Jesus said to give them food,
No one had enough.
Till one small boy gave up his lunch,
No one had enough.
With a small fish here
And a small loaf there,
Here a fish, there a loaf,
Jesus broke and blessed them.
When the miracle was done,
Everyone was filled.

Leader: There was a child who gave without worrying about being inadequate. May we be so filled with faith that we truly believe what we have to give can change the world. Amen!

People: Amen!

Exercise: Lessons Through Music

Begin this session by playing and listening to songs of faith for children from a variety of cultures and in a variety of languages. Music is an important means for teaching, and children as well as adults enjoy singing cheerful songs. Psalms were the songs of believers in ancient times. Look in the Scripture index in the back of The United *Methodist Hymnal, pp. 923-924, to locate some Psalms set to more recent music. Singing the Psalms is a good way to memorize Scripture and learn its life-giving message. Which songs would children enjoy singing? Have the group sing a phrase from a Psalm or set a Bible story to the tune "Row, Row, Row Your Boat" or some other familiar tune.*

Exercise: Lessons for Life in God

Leader: This last session addresses how we teach children and how they teach us. The Bible gives great emphasis to the importance of passing on our faith to the children, teaching them about God's will and purpose for our lives. For both God's chosen people in the Old Testament and the early Christians, being able to preserve the faith was an urgent matter. In Deuteronomy, it was urged that the children be taught God's commandments day and night (Deut. 6:6-7), and Jesus admonished that we teach the children well lest we become stumbling blocks to them and suffer the consequences (Matt. 18:6-7).

How did we learn to study the Bible and to pray? Here is one example:

"My mother taught me to pray kneeling by the side of my bed, with the palms of my hands held together and my fingers pointing upwards as a sign of dependence on God. My grandmother taught me to read the Bible seated at her feet while she embroidered or knitted. She would choose the Scripture passage and I would read it for both of us. It was how I learned to read. After I had read the passage, she would ask me questions. What did the passage say to me? What was Jesus trying to teach us? What would we do differently because of what the Bible said? My mother and grandmother stand in the tradition of the women of Israel who carried the responsibility for teaching the children."

Those are the words of this study guide's author, Bishop Minerva Carcaño.

Have the participants take a few moments to remember how they first learned how to pray and to read and study the Scriptures. Provide sheets of white paper and a variety of colored markers or crayons. Invite the participants to draw themselves learning to pray and to study Scripture. After all have had an opportunity to prepare their drawings, invite the participants to share their drawings with two or three other people. Gather information about teaching children by asking the participants to do the following:

Name the person or people who taught you to pray and study Scripture.

Identify the teaching methods that were used to teach you.

Tell what the experience of learning to pray and study Scripture meant for you.

Have a group member jot down the participants' responses on a sheet of newsprint, a piece of poster board, or a chalkboard for later reference.

After all have shared their memories, have a discussion about how today's children can best be taught the Christian faith, including how to pray and study Scripture. Refer to the ways that the participants, themselves, learned the fundamentals of the Christian faith. What teaching methods still work today? What are the present-day challenges of teaching children the Christian faith?

Exercise: Stages of Faith Development
(6 Readers)

Leader: James Fowler, an expert in faith development, has made a highly important contribution to the church's task of teaching the faith by helping us understand the way we learn. Fowler's six stages of faith make it clear that children's ways of learning differ from adults' ways.

Although infancy is not a separate stage, Fowler describes the time between birth and approximately two years of age as a period when children are learning how to trust. Though some recent research may prove this to be wrong, it is presently held that language and conceptual thought are not yet possible at this age. But, with or without complex language or conceptual thought, Fowler argues that infancy is the stage when we form our basic sense of trust in others and even begin to develop pre-images of God and the kind of world we live in. We build our faith on this foundation of trust or lack of trust, depending on what we have experienced.

Here is a summary of Fowler's six stages.

Reader 1: *Intuitive/Projective Faith*—Children between the ages of 3 and 7 generally fall into this stage. Children begin to develop an imagination but lack the capacity to use logic to question their perceptions or fantasies. Powerful experiences and images of faith take form in a child's mind.

Reader 2: *Mythic/Literal Faith*—A child of 8 to 11 years of age begins to be able to engage the world and find meaning in life. At this stage, children begin to evaluate the perceptions and fantasies they had at the previous stage. They are moved by stories and can form and retell stories that have touched them, though children are generally not yet fully ready to reflect on the meaning of the stories.

Reader 3: *Synthetic/Conventional Faith*—In this third stage, 12- and 13-year-old adolescents begin to think about their own thinking. Young people become concerned about forming an identity and are sensitive to the feedback they receive from those closest to them. At this stage, God is known personally, often experienced as a friend or companion. Fowler's use of the word *synthetic* in this stage means a pulling together, or synthesis, of one's images, values, and sense of self or identity.

Reader 4: *Individuative/Projective Faith*—This stage is usually reached between the ages of 17 and 25, though some people are not able to reach this stage until they are in their late 30s and others never leave the faith stage of adolescence.

In this fourth stage, we learn how to move out of the comfort of the circle of family and friends who have taught and nurtured us to this point in order to live our lives with authenticity and conviction about what we believe. This stage is concerned about boundaries: Where do I stop and you begin? Where do the groups that I belong to end and others begin?

Reader 5: *Conjunctive Faith*—In stage five, we become more aware of the fact that life is not just about clear boundaries. Much of life is somewhat porous and ever-changing. At this stage, we become more aware of our unconscious self and are generally more ready to welcome the God of mystery, whose nature is beyond our comprehension.

Reader 6: *Universalizing Faith*—Fowler believes that only a few devout people reach this stage. He describes it as one in which people take the radical step of living their faith as if the kingdom of God were already a fact. The core of a person's being becomes participation in God's ultimate reality. People negate the self for the sake of affirming God.

(Adapted from James Fowler, *Stages of Faith: The Psychology of Human Development and the Quest for Meaning*, New York: Harper Collins, 1981.)

Divide the group into three smaller groups and, using Fowler's stages of faith development, ask each group to work out an appropriate and helpful way to teach the following biblical children to pray and to study Scripture:

Group 1	*Ishmael and Isaac*
Group 2	*The Widow's Son of I Kings 17*
Group 3	*Jairus's Daughter*

Once the small groups have developed their teaching plans, have each one teach the entire group as if the class *represented the biblical child or children they prepared to teach. After all three small groups have taught the class, discuss the teaching sessions. Have participants assist each other to improve and to accommodate their plans for teaching children back home.*

Exercise: Learning to Teach, Learning to Care

Leader: Dr. Michael Warren, a religious educator who has committed much of his life to ministry with young people, believes that genuine care for young people is based on fidelity. He writes:

> "I believe that fidelity to young people in our time begins with a quality of care, of perceivable care, in those who would seek to influence them towards good. The importance of adult influence born of care appears to be especially significant in our day, when we see an epidemic of self-destructive behavior among teens."

(Michael Warren, *Youth Gospel Liberation*, New Rochelle, NY: Veritas Press, 1998, p. 90.)

As the church, we may very well need to learn anew how to create a culture of care for our young people and children in order to share with them the good news of God's love for them. To do this, we may need to invite children and young people to teach us how we might act effectively.

Have your panel of child experts speak to the group about what they would like to see the church do to help them learn about God better. Enter into conversation with your panelists. If you have video- or audiotaped your panel, then discuss what you hear the children saying to you. What changes must the church make to be faithful to God's call to care for the children?

Closing

Enter into a time of prayers of petition and thanksgiving for children. Ask participants to lift up concerns about children whom they know personally and for children in the world. Invite the participants to respond to each petition with the words, "Hear us, O God."

Then move into a time of lifting up prayers of thanksgiving for children and the many things and ways they contribute to life. Participants can respond to each prayer with the words, "Thanks be to God."

Video Meditation: "Children of Hope"
This five-minute video is available from the Service Center; telephone: 800-305-9857.

Closing Song: Repeat the song with which we began our study, "Jesus Loves the Little Children," p. 91.

Blessing

Leader: Children are our lifeline!

People: May the children prosper and live long and fruitful lives!

Leader: We are the caregivers that God has given the children of the world.

People: May God give us wisdom, compassionate hearts, and courageous spirits, as we seek to be faithful to God's charge.

Leader: What are the children?

People: They are our lifeline!

All: Thanks be to God for all the children of the world!

Additional Resources:

UNICEF website for youth, "Voices of Youth": http://www.unicef.org/voy/

UNICEF website on children of the world: http://www.unicef.org/

THE AUTHORS

Stephanie Biggs-Scribner is currently working on her Ph.D. in Hebrew Bible at Brite Divinity School in Fort Worth, Texas. She holds an MA in Bible from Jewish Theological Seminary of America and a BA in Religion from Oklahoma City University, a United Methodist partner institution. She has written for *Response* magazine, a publication of the Women's Division, General Board of Global Ministries. Expressing the quality of her relationship with her husband, the Rev. Lee Biggs-Scribner, she affectionately describes him as her partner in life. Lee is an ordained deacon and has supported her through her devastating diagnosis with multiple sclerosis and the symptoms she's experienced thus far. Stephanie was 28 and just beginning her Ph.D. studies when she experienced her first "exacerbation" and received her diagnosis. Stephanie and Lee are raising their daughter, Maggie Elisabeth, to be a dedicated member of The United Methodist Church and UMW. They stress to her the value of questioning Things—not just accepting things as they are.

Maggie Elisabeth Biggs-Scribner was 10 years old when she wrote these letters with her mother. She is now an 11-year-old sixth grader studying oboe, taking accelerated classes in her local public school, Chisholm Trail Intermediate, and playing both goalie and forward positions in soccer. Maggie's favorite foods are Mexican food (Tex-Mex), seafood, and spaghetti. Her favorite things to do are play soccer and watch science fiction programs like SG-1. She has lived in Oklahoma, New York, and Texas and has traveled internationally to Canada, Mexico, and South Korea—which was her favorite! Maggie hopes to study as a foreign exchange student to Germany in high school, but she will miss her two cats, Francis and Pippi, a three-legged part-Siamese black cat, and her beloved dog, Sugar. Sugar is an American Shar-Pei/Husky/Shepherd mix. Maggie is glad she took the time to write these letters. She says: "It gave me a whole other world to explore. It gave me something else to see and endure that most kids don't get to." Maggie also said that she liked the experience of working with her mother.

The Rev. Dr. Linda H. Hollies is founder and director of WomanSpace, Inc. She is directing the 2004-2005 class for Women's Leadership Institute, a partnership program with Western Theological Seminary. Linda is an ordained clergywoman in The United Methodist Church who studied under Rosemary Radford Reuther and Emily Townes at Garrett-Evangelical Theological Seminary. She is a nationally known author of more than 20 books, including: *Inner Healing for Broken Vessels* (Upper Room Books), *Taking Back My Yesterdays* (Pilgrim Press), and *Jesus and Those Bodacious Women* (Pilgrim Press).

Bishop Minerva G. Carcaño is the first Hispanic clergywoman to be elected to that position in The United Methodist Church. She has a master's degree from Perkins School of Theology, Southern Methodist University, and a bachelor's degree with a specialization in social work from the University of Texas—Pan American in Edinburg. With a wide-ranging history of service in The United Methodist Church, she was previously the superintendent of the Metropolitan District of the Oregon-Idaho Conference. From 1996 to 2001, she served as director of the Mexican-American Program and the Hispanic Studies Program, was coordinator of the Spanish

(continued on next page)

Language Section of the Course of Study School, and was adjunct faculty at Perkins School of Theology, Southern Methodist University, Dallas. Bishop Carcaño has also been a district superintendent in the Rio Grande Conference and an organizing pastor in Albuquerque, N.M. From 1979 to 1992, she was pastor of local churches throughout Texas, and between 1979 and 1986, she served churches in Texas and California. She was a director of the former United Methodist Board of Education and has served as a director on the United Methodist Board of Global Ministries, the United Methodist Board of Church and Society, and the United Methodist Publishing House. She served on two General Conference commissions—Our Theological Task and the Connectional Process Team—and on the South Central and Western Jurisdictions' Korean ministry councils. She was a delegate to the 1996 and 2004 General Conferences and to the 1998 World Council of Churches Assembly in Zimbabwe, Africa.